A Devotional Daybook

by Neva Coyle

When Life Takes More Than It Gives

Discovering God's Care When
You've Given All You Can

BETHANY HOUSE PUBLISHERS

MINNEAPOLIS, MINNESOTA 55438

Published by Bethany House Publishers
A Ministry of Bethany Fellowship, Inc.
11300 Hampshire Avenue South
Minneapolis, Minnesota 55438

Printed in the United States of America.

Library of Congress Cataloging-in-Publication Data

Coyle, Neva
    When life takes more than it gives / Neva Coyle.
        p.   cm. — (Devotional daybook)
    ISBN 1–55661–589–2 (pbk.)
      1. Encouragement—Religious aspects—Christianity—Meditations.
2. Devotional calendars. I. Title. II. Series: Coyle, Neva, 1943–
Devotional daybook.
BV4647.E53C6   1996
242—dc20   96–10064
                                                      CIP

When Life Takes More Than It Gives

Discovering God's Care When
You've Given All You Can

Nonfiction Books by Neva Coyle

Abiding Study Guide
Daily Thoughts on Living Free
Diligence Study Guide
Discipline tape album (4 cassettes)
Free to Be Thin, The All-New (with Marie Chapian)
Free to Be Thin Lifestyle Plan, The All-New
Free to Be Thin Cookbook
Free to Be Thin Daily Planner
Free to Dream
Freedom Study Guide
Learning to Know God
Living by Chance or by Choice
Living Free
Living Free Seminar Study Guide
Making Sense of Pain and Struggle
Meeting the Challenges of Change
A New Heart . . . A New Start
Obedience Study Guide
Overcoming the Dieting Dilemma
Perseverance Study Guide
Restoration Study Guide
Slimming Down and Growing Up (with Marie Chapian)
There's More to Being Thin Than Being Thin (with Marie
    Chapian)

9607

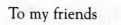

To my friends

Preface

IN A RAPIDLY GROWING and changing church, I was asked to take over the supervision of the departmental ministries. How exciting and what a creative challenge! Finding the opportunity just up my alley, I rolled up my sleeves and dug in. Within months I saw my area of responsibility humming along smoothly. The departmental coordinators responded well to the changes, and tighter organizational controls made everybody's job easier. Then new ministries began forming, and my task enlarged to include the recruitment and training of new leaders. As we moved into new and larger facilities, logistics became a hot-button item, as did coordinating the church calendar. Overseeing the church newsletter and weekly bulletin was added to my growing list of tasks. One day I woke up and realized I could hardly put my feet on the floor before my phone began ringing with an insistent, urgent caller on the other end.

I hadn't realized until that moment how tired I had become—tired of the endless duties that were at first so exciting. Instead of being a wonderful challenge and opportunity for ministry, the endless meeting of others' needs and demands had become burdensome. Life was taking a lot more than it was giving back. Without knowing it, that early morning caller had alerted me to the truth. Sadly, unintentionally, I had let God's work come between me and God. I was busy making sure everything happened nicely and orderly so that others could reach Him, but at what cost to me?

I can't tell you when it got out of hand. I can't specifically point to the day when it suddenly became overwhelming. But I can tell you this: what started out to be challenging and exciting, helping administrate ten departments, had become overburdening and threatening when two years later it had grown to twenty-four departments and intrachurch ministries.

Fortunately, this crisis came to a reasonable and practical solution when the job was divided and distributed among others. But afterward I was left wondering, "How does this happen to me? This isn't the first time I've gotten in over my head. How do I manage to get myself into these situations?" Am I an unreasonable, incurable overachiever? Hardly. Do I like adding stress to my already stressful life? Not on your life. I seem to stumble into these situations blindly, often willingly, and find that while I'm producing, I'm also tiring. While I'm holding up my end, I can come to feel as though no one is holding up *me*. And I've learned there are many people, whether they admit it or not, who do the same thing.

Increasing responsibilities in our lives can slowly creep up on us and get out of control before we even realize what is happening. Sometimes we can alleviate the problem by delegating some of our work—as I finally did at our church. But there are other situations in life that demand much more of us than we have to give, and there simply seems to be no way out. We may, for example, be unexpectedly thrown into a crisis situation where we must provide round-the-clock care for someone we love. At such times, even the everyday duties that are normally quite manageable can suddenly become unmanageable. And when that daily care must continue on and on, we can feel that we're reaching the end of our rope and wonder where God has gone.

I am also deeply acquainted with this kind of situation,

where additional responsibilities simply cannot be avoided or delegated, but must be accepted as God's choice for us. Yet even when we can accept God's will in our circumstances, we may find ourselves so tired out by the unrelenting demands that we become drained of our energy and joy— just barely making it through the endless drudgery of caring for others.

What do you do when every day is heavy going? When responsibilities and caregiving activities foist nothing but endless duties and continual demands on you? What do you do when life unrelentingly goes on even though you sense you are at the end of your ability to endure and cope?

Life takes more than it gives in many ways. Long after others have forgotten, there are those who can recall a long-ago personal crisis as if it were yesterday because they face daily the devastating debris it has left in their life. Some can never quite recover from the disappointment and disillusionment of a marriage that is certainly less than was promised at the beginning. Others face the care of an elderly, perhaps even ungrateful or bitter, parent. Some face lifetime commitments to caring for a sibling or child who was born with less than the necessary abilities to care for themselves. People who have experienced shattered hopes and have had their lives come to a sudden stop may be able to identify the exact moment their burdens began to pile up but can't figure out how to unload them.

Most of us have had those moments when a sinking feeling told us something was very wrong: a flash of realization that signaled, "I have nothing to show for all my hard work or faithfulness." Still others will admit to an unquenched thirst or unfulfilled longing deep within. Many carry the essence of an unanswered prayer or know the heart sickness caused by a deferred hope.

Long after a crisis, even when safer ground is once again reached and life returns to a reestablished routine, life has to go on. The sudden seriousness of a tragically ill mate can turn into years of perpetual care and unending responsibility. And when we've moved beyond the initial tears, and even when necessary adjustments have been made, many women just like you and me find that the luster of our lives is gone,

9

and instead of a vibrant daily life, we push through a daily grind.

And we get tired. Tired of the situation, tired of our responsibilities, and tired of being tired.

But does this have to be a part of our daily reality? Do failure and disappointment, as well as overwhelming responsibilities and unending duties, have to leave indelible tracks across our hearts and show forever in our faces?

Can our hearts ever be continually thankful again? Can our eyes sparkle and the spring return to our steps when our situations refuse to change? Can the energy of pure joy return to our thoughts and prayers even when life continues to extract much more than it returns? Can we learn how to win over the bitter battles that threaten our lives and peace?

Are you finding that life has taken more than it has returned? This fifth book in the DEVOTIONAL DAYBOOK series is written specifically for you. It is designed to help you—right in the middle of your taxing responsibilities—find the peace and joy that has slipped from your attitudes and outlook. It points the way to the source of real and lasting hope, trust, and satisfaction through the truth of God's Word.

After each daily devotional reading, ask yourself the questions and write down your answers. Then, with God's help, you can apply these newly or rediscovered truths of God's Word to your life, your heart, and your circumstances. You can soon experience the refreshing touch of God's love and healing to your heart. And while your circumstances may never change—you will. And your responsibilities? They won't go away simply because you read this book.

But could you use more strength in handling them? Would you like some help in carrying the burdens that weigh so heavily on your shoulders? Then this book is for you. My prayers are filled with tenderness for the readers who are drawn by the title, and whose lives require more than they feel capable of giving. May God bless you as you begin and sustain you as you continue. And may He also return to you what you have selflessly given to others.

Contents

Introduction: How to Use This Book 13

Section I • Come Into His Presence 15

1. When God Calls 17
2. Unmasking 21
3. But As for Me 25
4. Abiding 29
5. Standing on the Rock 33

Section II • Let Down Your Guard 37

6. Run to the Name of the Lord 39
7. Drop Into the Everlasting Arms 43
8. Search Me, Lord 47
9. Shelter From the Storm 51
10. Sustained by His Mercy 55

Section III • Open Your Heart 59

11. After All I've Done for You! 61
12. Beyond the Heart of the Matter 65

13. The Accessible Heart 69
14. The Available Heart 73
15. The Teachable Heart 77

Section IV • Let God Love You 83

16. Love Without Measure 85
17. Nurturing the Seed of God's Love 89
18. God's Reaching Love 93
19. An Endless Reservoir of Love 97
20. A New Perspective 101

Section V • Listen to His Voice 105

21. The Voice That Refreshes 107
22. The Voice That Gives New Life 111
23. The Voice That Calms........................... 115
24. The Voice That Comforts........................ 119
25. The Voice That Is With You Always 123

Section VI • Rest in Him 127

26. Trusting the God of Our Past, Present, and Future 129
27. God's Transcending Peace 133
28. A Royal Legacy 137
29. To All Who Are Weary 141
30. Beside Quiet Waters 147

Leader's Notes 151

How to Use This Book

THIS DEVOTIONAL STUDY is designed to fit easily into a busy schedule. It is divided into six sections, with five chapters in each section. By reading a chapter each day, you can complete the study in just thirty days. Take a few minutes each day to read the suggested Scripture. Apply the Scripture selection to your life by answering the questions at the end of each chapter. Writing your own response in the space after the questions will help you better establish the scriptural truths in your life.

If the book is used in a group study, members can study the five chapters of a section during the week and then meet as a group to discuss the material. In this way the book will take six weeks to complete, or longer, depending on the needs of the group. The study is easily adaptable to an established women's ministry group or a Sunday school class.

For groups using the study, suggested leader's guidelines and discussion questions are included at the end of the book.

Section I

Come Into His Presence

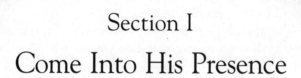

Come to me, all you who are weary and burdened, and I will give you rest. Take my yoke upon you and learn from me, for I am gentle and humble in heart, and you will find rest for your souls. For my yoke is easy and my burden is light.

MATTHEW 11:28–30

IMAGINE ADAM AND EVE in the Garden immediately after they had sinned. Can you feel their panic and dread as they heard God approaching?

"The man and his wife heard the sound of the LORD God as he was walking in the garden in the cool of the day, and they hid from the LORD God among the trees of the garden. But the LORD God called to the man, 'Where are you?'

He answered, 'I heard you in the garden, and I was afraid because I was naked; so I hid' "(Genesis 3:8–10).

Ever feel like that? One day you're enjoying God's presence, and *wham!* the next day you're wanting to hide from everyone and everybody—*including God!*

I have felt that way. Stripped emotionally naked, unable to face my responsibilities, and even avoiding my quiet time. How sad and what a mistake. God has been wanting us to live unashamed in His presence—and to come for inner refreshing—since the beginning of time. To be able to come to Him with our lives and hearts exposed completely. But we do it backward. We think we have to come to Him already filled, cheery, smiling.

For the next five days, our focus will center on this first, essential aspect of living lives that exact more than they return—entering His presence.

Chapter
· 1 ·

When God
Calls

Read Exodus 3:1–4.
Reflect on these words from verse 4:

God called to him from within the bush, "Moses! Moses!"
And Moses said, "Here I am."

It never fails. Just when I need the time to be left alone
to tend to my responsibilities, somebody calls. I have a way,
however, of helping me deal with such untimely interruptions—an answering machine. My own prerecorded voice
cheerfully greets the caller and invites them to either call
later, or leave their message and I'll get back to them at another time.

Unfortunately, I have become aware that I've brought
the convenience of the electronic answering machine into
my prayer life, and, sadly, it has affected the way I relate to
God as well. I know it's hard to believe, but it's true.

Here's what I look like sometimes. There I am, the busy
"home executive," swooshing through my days. A little
"ring" sounds inside. My soul, like a dutiful secretary, says,
"God's on the line. He needs to talk to you."

"Hold my calls," I bark, ignoring my secretary. I sweep
past her desk. "No interruptions!"

How many times have you said, "Not now, God. Too
many responsibilities to tend to. We'll have to talk later,
when I've finished here"? Or do you—as I sometimes do—

want to know what's on God's mind *before* you respond, so you try to find a way to screen God's call? Maybe if we could just find some clever way to stay out of touch . . . within hearing, mind you, but legitimately out of reach. Of course, our very best intention is to get back to God as soon as possible—or at least when it's more convenient.

It's not that unusual as we struggle to keep all the pieces of our lives together to want to protect ourselves from further "assignments," or from having the Holy Spirit speak to us about a bad attitude or critical spirit. Looking at our limited resources and the pressure of our present responsibilities, we shake our heads and wonder what more could God possibly want or expect of us.

Even when we're overwhelmed with the realities of our day-to-day lives, "up to here" with the demands of others' needs, or even hindered from what we sense God's "real" purpose is for us—even then we avoid God's call, when we need His touch the most. When we'd die for a simple whisper of appreciation or nod of encouragement, we shrink from God's voice, afraid to even take the chance of listening because He might want something more than we're already giving. Hard-pressed to remember the last time we truly enjoyed ourselves in God's presence, we simply push some inward control button. *I'll return your call as soon as possible.*

However, the day of facing Him and listening to what He has to say can't be postponed forever. Somewhere deep inside, beyond self-protection and emotional fatigue, is a driving need to be with the Father—an inner hunger that longs to be fed by His words and love. In those precious moments alone with God, if you and I expect a stern rebuke for not *doing* more, *giving* more, or *being* more—when we're already stretched beyond our limits—we have sadly underestimated God's love and care for us.

Not every call of God has more work attached to it. Not every call comes from a burning bush, either. Most likely, it will come from a deep, familiar spot of cold loneliness or burning frustration. And it will come not as an interruption, but as *intervention*—the Father involving himself in our lives, keeping us in His constant care.

As frequently as we involve ourselves with our routine

18

daily activities, so too would the Father involve himself with us. As close as the carpet under our feet as we walk through the day, the spatula in our hands as we prepare the evening meal, or the steering wheel in our cars as we navigate our way to our usual daily appointments, God is just as near . . . calling us by name as He did Moses. Isn't it time we responded as Moses did: "Here I am, Lord"?

Chances are God will not be asking you to lead an entire nation out of bondage and slavery, but He may well speak to you about your own freedom and liberty. Maybe He'll address your lack of joy, or how to regain the gladness you thought you had lost forever. Perhaps He'd simply like to love you up close and personal again . . . or speak to you about the load you are carrying and assure you of His care and concern.

I ask you to turn off your "inner answering machine" and take this call now. Let the rest of life wait until you can get back to it, knowing how much you need these few minutes alone with the Father.

For the next few days, I invite you to do something quite on purpose. Take a few minutes each day and, like Moses, go investigate what the Lord wants to say through this simple book. Let the message come alive as you reflect on God's Word, and ask yourself the questions posed. Then in an attitude of prayerful reflection, respond in writing to the Lord as He speaks to you. And to do that, all you need to say is, "Here I am."

God is whispering your name. He desperately wants to reach you. Will you let Him?

What load are you carrying that tends to interfere with hearing God's voice clearly?

What do you deal with on a regular basis that makes you dread hearing God whisper your name?

What will you have to leave untended until later if you plan a time to be alone with God for a few minutes each morning?

Are you willing to set down and leave until later those things listed above to give yourself personal time with the Savior?

Write your decision in the form of a prayer.

Chapter · 2 ·

Unmasking

Read James 4:7–10.
Reflect on these words from verse 8:

"Come near to God and he will come near to you."

Perhaps you are like me, perhaps not. But I have to honestly admit there are some days I'd like to run away. Ever feel like that? Sometimes the inner pressure can become so intense I think I'll explode. Tears push against the top of my emotional dam, straining it beyond its strength. Once they start, I'm afraid they'll never stop. But I have learned to cope—or have I? I have learned to maintain a facade of laughter and humor. I've actually learned to do and say the right things even when inside I'm falling apart. Pile it on; I can take it. But don't be kind to me—oh, please, don't be too kind. You see, it's easier to give comfort than to receive it. I can't maintain my faux-strength then.

Wouldn't it be nice if there were a room somewhere in the church—padded and insulated to make it soundproof—where we could go and let it all out? A safe place to let loose, to scream to our heart's content, to unload our frustration once and for all? A psychologist might tell us that it would lighten our load and make us feel better.

But in the long run would it help all that much?

Reread the words of James 4:7–8. Can we actually believe them? Can we believe that if we "resist" the devil he will "flee" from us? Or do we think we could never be "close" enough to God for this to happen? But the promise is clear, and it's for every one of us. "Come near to God and He will come near to you." And there's more. Read on—close to God is where we can wash our hands clean of bad attitudes and pick our souls clean of unwanted lint and dirt. It's where our hearts can be washed clean, clear through. And it's where we can let it all out—safely, securely, let it all out.

This is where we don't have to be strong for anybody; we can remove our masks and face our emotions honestly. The gloom so secretly harbored can be unlocked and released. Here, safely in God's presence, we can let the dam burst, give voice to our sorrow, vent our anger. God is here, and He can take it.

He has invited *you* to this place—this safe place.

And for what? Just to give you some badly needed emotional release? Hardly.

This is the place where you can humble yourself, admit your shortcomings, face your fears, be honest about your inadequacies. But more than that, it is the place where He would speak to you at a depth you could not hear Him before.

Are you ready? Listen:

Do not think your labor unnoticed
    Or unseen your sorrow and pain.
Have I not promised to wipe every teardrop?
    To lighten unbearable burdens and then,
Though weeping continue all through the night,
    Have I not promised joy with morning light?
(Based on Psalm 30:5; Isaiah 25:8)

———

If you felt free to approach God honestly and openly with the most painful or frustrating issue of your entire life, what would that issue be?

If you openly poured out your heart to God about your current responsibilities or demanding burdens, what would you want to say?

In what ways do you pretend to be strong when you're not?

How can you let God help you with His strength?

What is the Lord saying to you today? (Listen for a few minutes before you answer this.)

Now, in the quietness of this moment, pick up—no, no, not those old masks and facades—but His peace and strength. Face your day with His reassurance and love. Leave the costumes you wore in here behind. You won't need to play any other role than your real self today. You don't need any masks or facades for that, do you?

For added reassurance, read Hebrews 10:22–23: "Let us draw near to God with a sincere heart in full assurance of faith, having our hearts sprinkled to cleanse us from a guilty conscience and having our bodies washed with pure water. Let us hold unswervingly to the hope we profess, for he who promised is faithful."

Chapter · 3 ·

But As for Me . . .

Read Psalm 73:21–28.
Reflect on these words from verse 28:

> *"But as for me, it is good to be near God. I have made the Sovereign LORD my refuge."*

But as for me . . . How long has it been since you actually considered what was in *your* best interest? Perhaps in the day-to-day demands of your responsibilities you have become so accustomed to what is good for others that you have overlooked the importance of also remembering what is good for you.

Bobbi didn't know this was happening to her. Healthy, energetic, and intelligent, she was well on her way to a satisfying career in banking. Then, at thirty, she happily left the workplace to stay home and care for her family. The busy mother of two active boys barely a year apart, she found it easy to immerse herself in their lives. The boys were both in the gifted program at school and were active in all kinds of sports and church activities. Soon Bobbi wasn't just their mother, but the team mother, room mother, and den mother. Even her gift of hospitality was often used for entertaining her ambitious husband's clients or prospective agents. At first she found all this activity stimulating, but at some point she realized she was on a treadmill she couldn't stop. Overbusy, overcommitted, and soon overtired, she became a missing person without leaving home. You see, in taking care of everyone else, she forgot to take care of herself.

The same could be said of Dorothy. The oldest of five siblings, and the one living nearest to her mother, it was the most natural thing to do to make room for Mom when she became unable to take care of herself. After all, it had been the family's pattern for generations. But caring for her mother is not Dorothy's only responsibility. She also cares for her disabled husband, and is raising a teenage granddaughter, not to mention the fact that she runs a small home business. Extraordinary caregiving demands crept up on her one at a time, leaving Dorothy with little time and energy for her own needs.

Dictated both by circumstance and my personal nature, I too am a caregiver. When my husband became unable to work, it seemed natural for me to slip into a more prominent role. As his helpmeet, I not only became his caregiver, but the major wage earner and family provider. I try to balance the needs of others with my own, but when it becomes too overwhelming—simply too much work—I can all too easily fall into the same trap that Bobbi and Dorothy have encountered. I can simply give up on seeing that my own needs are met, too tired to do anything about it. Then, just before I snap, something clicks in my mind: "But as for me . . ."

But as for me . . . It sounds selfish when somebody else's needs are so evident, and the responsibility for their care falls directly on my shoulders. *But as for me . . .* is a luxury I can hardly afford—or is it?

"But as for me," the Bible says, "it is good to be near God." There are those whose lives are so wrapped up in the caring of others that the last thing they want when they finally get a moment's reprieve is to be close to *anyone*. Even lunch with the girls or a day shopping with a close friend is too taxing. *I just want to be alone! Surely God understands.*

And He does! If you are living with extreme demands on your time and energies, finding some quiet moments of solitude is a healthy step in caring for your own needs. But in those moments of refuge, don't make the mistake of thinking that God is a threat or an intrusion to that refuge. He *is* your refuge!

Those of us who must carry heavy demands every day need to learn how to be refreshed in God. When we choose to walk only in our own strength, depending on ourselves alone in our moments of refuge, we don't go back to our responsibilities recharged in anything but *ourselves*. That's self-defeating!

By leaving God out of the picture, we open ourselves to the devil's lies and are quickly defeated in our thought life. "Coming near to God" is part of the prescription for "resisting" the devil. When I am especially battered and bruised by what the devil wants me to believe, the last person I need to turn to for help and restoration is *me*. Usually by this time, my mind is so filled with sour thoughts that being alone with myself can make matters worse. I'm pooped, I'm too close to my situation to be objective, and I'm empty. It is the Lord I need to turn to for refuge. He never tires, He always sees the bigger picture, and He overflows with new life, energy, and wisdom—all of which He desires to give to me.

Running into His safe and secure presence, I find safer ground to pause and reflect. When left alone in my own presence I frequently overreact. But I have discovered something else quite wonderful: it's okay not to react, or even respond to certain things, until I've been able to take them first into His presence for refuge-reflection. Yes, that's right, to actually delay my response until I have had a moment with the Master. I call it a *thinking delay*. An I'll-think-about-it-tomorrow kind of attitude that some might call procrastination, or even a little melodramatic. But listen: I know what it's like to be so tired and weary that everything you do you question, every decision you make you second-guess . . . when every challenge is met with a reaction instead of a well-thought-through response . . . when every suggestion is interpreted as criticism and every discussion becomes an argument. That's when I know I need to run somewhere for safety, and I've learned that time by myself with *me* isn't going to give me what I need.

"But as for me," we all need to learn to say, "it is good to be near God. I have made the Sovereign LORD my refuge."

27

If you were to be totally honest, when was the last time you actually considered, "But as for *me . . .*"?

How do you convince yourself you don't need to be with the Lord for moments of precious and needed refuge?

What do you need to tell yourself in order to be convinced that your moments with Him are exactly what you need?

How can you give yourself permission to go into God's presence on a regular basis and make the Sovereign Lord your own personal refuge?

Chapter · 4 ·

Abiding

Read John 15:1–8.
Reflect on these words from verses 4 and 5:

> *"Remain in me, and I will remain in you. No branch can bear fruit by itself; it must remain in the vine. Neither can you bear fruit unless you remain in me. I am the vine; you are the branches. If a man remains in me and I in him, he will bear much fruit; apart from me you can do nothing."*

"Out here on my own, all alone with no one to care. . . ." Yikes! What a familiar song! What a trap—and it's waiting, loaded with bait and ready to spring on all of us. No kidding. Let me ask you a couple of questions.

How long has it been since *you* exhaled a long sigh of contentment or felt a bottomless source of peace and satisfaction? When was the last time your heart virtually rang with a spontaneous song of delight?

Is your life more likely to be filled with moments when you have to fight hard against the tears and simply refuse to let them fall? Do you more often have to gird yourself with resolve just to make it through one more tough hour? Instead of lifting your head in spontaneous praise and laughter, do you have to lift your chin and set your shoulders just to meet the challenge of your responsibilities head on?

If so, then you and I have much in common. And, if the parallel of our lives holds true, then you'll know what I'm talking about when I say that sometimes my responses to my responsibilities hold a note of impatience. You'll understand when I confess that if I'm not careful, my humor can become tinged with sarcasm, and I can grow generally resentful of my entire situation.

And can you also identify with the guilt I feel about my negative attitudes and the self-chastening about my own shortcomings, which can eventually lead to bitterness toward those who are dependent upon me?

If we're not careful, we caregivers can be left sitting out on a limb—certainly not experiencing *abiding in the vine* as described in John 15:4–5.

So, we've faced harsh realities before. Let's have the courage to face one more.

The truth is, we haven't died on the vine; we've simply allowed ourselves to be separated from it. It wasn't intentional, we just weren't attentive to what was happening. You see, we can accept God-given responsibilities as if they are something to *go* and do rather than *abide* or *stay* and do. We behave as though we are to do what God asks, and then come back to Him later. And, sadly, many of us don't understand why doing what we know God has given us to do seems to separate us from Him. Even our logic tells us that if we're doing God's work it ought to bring us closer to Him—certainly not take us farther away. And it never enters our mind, when we are unable to juggle everyone else's needs and still pay attention to our own, that we might be doing more than God has actually assigned. What about the times we take on those "extra" tasks of our own choosing? Do we even take the time to consider that "but as for me" may include letting go of some of our work—yes, even the "ministry" we are convinced no one else can do?

The secret of not only surviving but thriving through these difficult assignments is to realize how important our moments spent in maintaining our "vine life" are. More than important—they are crucial.

The invitation isn't just to come near to Him occasionally or drop in once in a while. It is to live united, joined, connected to God's love and presence day in and day out. Kept in His love and care moment by moment is the only way we can be sure that His love is pouring through us to those He's given us to care for in His name.

Don't worry; having God's presence isn't the same as having another person to care for and give attention to—it's more like having your own personal life-support system giving needed breath, hope, and love. It's having a tireless Caregiver of your own. A mere glance, a nod in His direction, and He extends His love and mercy toward you. Stay within His love; remain in Him. Without Him you can do nothing. United in Him, there is nothing you *can't* do.

———————

If you took a few minutes away from your responsibilities to tap into God's love and care for you, when would be the best time to plan for that?

What things would you have to do in preparation for a time spent with your own personal Caregiver, Jesus Christ?

What difference would it make in your attitudes if you knew God's care personally on a regular basis?

What difference would it make in how you relate to your responsibilities if you were aware of His constant care for you?

Write out your need and/or thanks in a prayer.

Now, exhale a long sigh of contentment in Christ's love. Feel the bottomless peace and satisfaction His care and concern offer. Is your heart longing to break out in songs of absolute delight? Have your circumstances changed? Probably not. But chances are *you* have.

Chapter
· 5 ·

Standing on
the Rock

Read Exodus 33:7–23.
Reflect on verses 14 and 21:

> *"The LORD replied, 'My Presence will go with you, and I will give you rest.' Then the LORD said, 'There is a place near me where you may stand on a rock.' "*

Imagine you are your own boss, giving yourself a performance review. How would you describe the quality of your daily work or caregiving lately? Would you say your employee (that's you!) exudes "an attractive air of calm and self-confidence that draws others like a magnet"? Or would you fill in the blank with "carries out responsibilities with quiet assurance, promoting peace and tranquillity in the lives of those she touches every day"? How about "adept at handling herself no matter what the challenge"? Or better yet, "responsibilities carried out cheerfully without tiresome, burdensome chains of doubt, impatience, or rudeness toward those who need her so much."

No? Me either.

The above descriptions are hardly what I'm like on a daily basis. But they do describe what I *think* I should be—come what may. Or at least what I'd *like* to be. Let's look at that imaginary performance review a bit closer.

The truth is, an "air of calm and self-confidence" doesn't necessarily draw others like a magnet. If it's an "act," it can actually push others away—making us appear unreachable. We can outwardly project an air of having it all together, while inwardly we're falling apart. Sometimes what may be perceived by others as calm and self-confidence may simply be an effort to hold it together after a sleepless night waiting for more medical test results, or holding on for dear life through another round of financial strain or harsh words. Okay, so you're not superhuman. That's all the more reason to come to a place, as Moses was commanded, where we can stand on solid rock—near God—and then come away not only with an "air" of calm and self-confidence, but with real peace and faith in His divine care and love. Yes, even in our difficult situations; even through our tears of doubt and frustration.

How many of us can actually "carry out unending responsibilities with quiet assurance, promoting peace and tranquillity in the lives of those we touch every single day"? Not many, if we're truthful. But from time to time we can. It's one thing, when you're called in an emergency, to rally to the situation, put your life on hold for the moment, and with quiet assurance handle the crisis with peace and tranquillity. But when that crisis doesn't end, when the breadwinner doesn't return to work, or the seizure-stricken child doesn't get better, only worse—what then? Do we force ourselves into thinking we must be "adept at handling" ourselves "no matter what the challenge"?

We'll never make it that way, my friend. The only way we will weather an "unending crisis" is by learning one important thing: God's presence has to be a dynamic that we not only return to frequently and with regularity, but also take with us back into the battle of our everyday, stress-filled lives. Only when we take the time—away, closed off, and apart from our responsibilities—will we be able to bring His presence back into those situations. I'm not talking about getting away for an expensive weekend at one of the "Great Country Inns." I'm simply pleading for you to stop begrudging yourself a five-to-twenty-minute break, a halfhour, or perhaps even an hour and a half each day. A break with one purpose in mind and one only: to be in God's presence. Not in the car on the way to work or running errands. Not while putting away another load of wash at midnight, sneaking in a prayer or two between folding socks and sheets. But setting aside time *exclusively* for the purpose of meeting with God—and nothing more. The snatches here and there are fine, but in addition to the time set apart for God alone.

Only then will reassurance and comfort be communicated in our touch, optimism and joy find their expression in our conversation, and new hope and energy splatter our outlook of the future with sunlight.

Only then can we carry out our responsibilities "cheerfully, without tiresome, burdensome chains of doubt, impatience, or rudeness toward those who need us so much."

Why? Because time apart with God will give us the assurance of His presence going with us—carrying us as we care for others in His name. And when you come to this new sense of a rock-solid place to stand near God, you will bring that rock-solid stability back to those who depend on you for care and love.

If you were to give yourself a performance review, what are the places of weakness and weariness that are evidently in need of God's touch and mercy?

If the tables were turned and *you* were the one receiving the constant care of another, how would you change what you perceive as your need? As theirs?

For a few moments put yourself in the shoes of someone you take care of every day. Imagine how they feel about you and all the things you do for them. Write down some of those things.

Are your comments negative or positive? What does this tell you about yourself?

Write a prayer asking God to help you step onto the solid rock of truth and view your situation from His perspective.

Section II

Let Down Your Guard

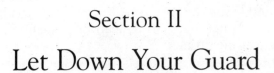

*P*ut on the full armor of God so that you can take your
stand against the devil's schemes. For our struggle is not
against flesh and blood, but against the rulers, against
the authorities, against the powers of this dark world
and against the spiritual forces of evil in the
heavenly realms. Therefore put on the full armor
of God, so that when the day of evil comes, you
may be able to stand your ground, and after
you have done everything, to stand."

EPHESIANS 6:11–13

DO YOU EVER FEEL like you will scream if you hear one more sermon on being strong? Do you ever feel like hanging it all up and being the weak one once? Or do you find yourself asking, "When do I get to lean on someone instead of everyone leaning on me?"

You're not alone.

That's why, with all the sermons and well-intended words to remain strong, to persevere, or to hang in there, we also need to remember that in God's presence we can step out of the armor and be our most vulnerable selves. That's right; there is a place to drop your guard and be perfectly safe at the same time.

These next five days, consider this idea. I promise you it will not strip away the strength you need to cope with your demanding life and overwhelming responsibilities. Just the opposite! You *have* the courage to be strong, to persevere, to continue. That's what you've been doing for so long. Now will you have the courage to leave all that behind for a few minutes—to open yourself up to the safety of God's presence?

Chapter · 6 ·

Run to the Name of the Lord

Read Isaiah 25:1–8.
Reflect on these words from Proverbs 18:10:

> *"The name of the LORD is a strong tower; the righteous run to it and are safe."*

"Come on, Neva," my friend pleaded. "What you need is a day out. We'll go shopping and out for lunch. We'll have a wonderful time. You really do need to be around more people—have more fun."

She was so right, but so very wrong at the same time. I did need to get away. But the last thing I needed was shopping, lunch, and fun. I needed rest and refuge. I needed a getaway that would help prepare me for the responsibilities that awaited me upon my return, a respite that would *re-energize* me for the tasks that would be left undone while I was away.

I also needed to be alone.

Alone where I could determine if I had really reached the limit of my energies, abilities, and coping skills; where I could admit that my once soft and spontaneous laugh had become a forced cackle; where I could face the fact that my sense of humor had developed a sharp edge of sarcasm, and that the demands of my day-to-day routine had indeed overtaken my usual sense of optimism and showered it with tears of hopelessness.

What I really needed was a sheltered, safe place where I could let down my hair—unleash my pent-up emotions and resentments.

A change of pace may invigorate the busy executive or overworked hairdresser, but a full-time caregiver needs more. Those whose lives have taken an unexpected turn—who find themselves with the full-on, no-getting-out-of-it responsibility of raising a grandchild, or caring for an elderly, sometimes difficult, parent, or a permanently or terminally ill spouse—need much more than a social event or day out shopping to restore them.

Caregivers like you and me don't need the mall; we need a miraculous moment of silence and solitude. We need quietness, where we can get back in touch with the inner softness we have protected or even buried deep within to avoid being hurt anymore. We long for the gentle silence where God's still, small voice of love and encouragement can be heard again . . . a brief period where we can feel safe enough to be vulnerable—secure enough to unwrap our raw emotions and expose them to God's healing touch.

Is there such a place? Is there time for such solitude?

I am happy to announce to you that this desperately needed moment of joyful respite is not only available; it is ready and waiting for you. And, believe it or not, it's as close as any burdensome or never-ending responsibility you carry at this very moment.

It's as close as the whispered name of our Lord Jesus Christ.

The promise of God's Word is this: "The name of the LORD is a strong tower; the righteous run to it and are safe."

Run to it. Simple, concise, and clear direction. Run to the name of the Lord: "Jesus." Go ahead, say it—"Jesus." Now say it again. Repeat it until you sense His lovely presence surround you like a warm and secure cocoon. Say it until the cobwebs of duty are cleared away, and the sparkling light of His wonderful care and concern for you shines through. Continue saying it until the demands of your life no longer entrap you emotionally, spiritually, and physically.

Then maintain your own inner retreat center by adding, "Thank You, Jesus. I love You, Jesus. You're my Lord."

Go ahead, run to the name of the Lord. Feel safe. Enjoy.

Now, the most wonderful miracle of all is this: Running to the name of the Lord not only gives us the strength we need to carry on, but also the energy to accept that lunch date with a friend. Yes, it's true. We retreat to the name of the Lord, and we reemerge into full life, once again able to carry out our responsibilities.

Read the promise again: *The name of the LORD is a strong tower; the righteous run to it and are safe.*

Ask yourself: How long has it been since I truly felt the Lord's strength?

How long since I truly felt safe?

How long since I took a few moments and *ran to the name of the Lord?*

Why not begin right now? Meditate on the name of the Lord and the refuge that is in it for you.

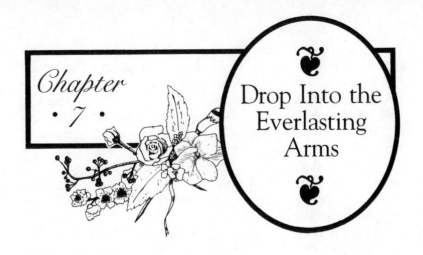

Chapter
· 7 ·

❦
Drop Into the Everlasting Arms
❦

Read Psalm 91.
Reflect also on these words from Deuteronomy 33:27:

"The eternal God is your refuge, and underneath are the everlasting arms."

Where do *I* go for support? So many depend on me; who do I depend on? Where is *my* leaning post?

It's so easy to get used to being the strong and responsible one, we forget that we too have needs and moments of weakness. Holding the reins of our lives so tightly, making sure that every detail gets covered, every errand accomplished, and every task completed on time takes the last ounce of strength and discipline we can muster. Letting go—dropping our guard—seems like suicide. Relaxing our stance even slightly feels like certain disaster. If only we can hang in there just a little longer, just until everything is "normal" again. We mustn't let go for even a minute or everything will fall apart!

An image comes to my mind of a woman who has fallen into a dark, dried-up well of undetermined depth. Clinging to the end of a rope, she holds on for dear life, yelling at the top of her lungs for help. Finally, when she has been hauled to the surface, her hands have to be pried from the death grip she has on the rope. One of her rescuers notes the approximate length of the rope and observes that it is nearly as long as the well is deep—short only by about the woman's height. Sure enough, a tape measure is dropped into the black hole and the rescuers determine that the woman was dangling only inches from the bottom. The whole time she was clinging for dear life, she could have been standing. She could have used her strength, or at least saved it, to assist in her own rescue when the time came.

"But," you say in her defense, "she didn't know."

No, she didn't. And neither do you or I until someone either illuminates our pit, or measures the rope while we dangle there.

That's what Deuteronomy 33:27 does for me. It shows me that I'm dangling barely above solid rock . . . that I can let go of the ropes of my life and drop, assured of the security that awaits only a hairsbreadth from my toes. It illuminates the emotional holes of my life and assures me there is a bottom to all of this. And that directly underneath me are the everlasting arms of my heavenly Father.

So when the emotional demands get too intense, I let myself drop. *Underneath me are the everlasting arms.* When financial strain assaults my security. *Underneath are the everlasting arms.* When circumstances and relationships are strained to their limits. When the needs of others have pushed me beyond my ability to cope, much less serve. *Underneath are the everlasting arms.* When I can't take any more—period. *Underneath are the everlasting arms.*

His name is a strong tower; I can run into it, be surrounded and safe. How wonderful! And now, if that weren't enough, I discover that underneath me are His everlasting arms. And they are there for you, too. Let go; let down your guard. Life may take more than it gives, but God is always there to give more . . . much more than life can ever take.

————

In what ways you do you hang on as if all of life's problems and circumstances depended on you?

44

What are some of the reasons you "hang in there" instead of letting go and dropping into the security of God's everlasting arms?

What is the emotional feeling you get when you think of letting down your guard and dropping an undetermined distance into God's hands?

If you were to let go and God *didn't* catch you, what areas of your life would most likely go completely out of control?

How can you learn to trust Him enough to let down your guard and rely on the promise that *underneath you are the everlasting arms?*

Chapter
· *8* ·

Search Me, Lord

Read Psalm 139.
Reflect on verse 23:

> *"Search me, O God, and know my heart; test me and know my anxious thoughts."*

"I hate it! I just hate it," one woman said. "I go to work every night telling myself I won't be like them. Being a Christian means I'm different; I treat the patients with tenderness and care. And, night after night, I'm not only bombarded with the needs of critically ill people, but also with the demands of foul-mouthed, filthy-minded co-workers."

Sound familiar? Maybe you're not in the medical field like my friend, but can you recognize what it means to work or live where you give more than you get day after day, month after month? Perhaps you have said the very same thing to yourself as my friend has said. Maybe you have braced yourself before you push open the door at work, or even at home or church.

"I'm different," you determine. "Jesus in me makes me different. I won't succumb to their mindless, loveless games. I'm not going to laugh at their dirty jokes or respond to their cutting remarks. I won't be like them; I just won't!"

Toughen up, we inwardly command ourselves. *Be strong!*

And, before we know it, we're resisting. A coping skill, of course. We put up walls. Defensive strategies, we tell our-

47

selves—appropriate and needed. We stay at arm's length—a survival technique. And in our attempt to be impervious, unaffected, and immune to the trash our circumstances hurl at us, we become callous and desensitized. Then, if we're not careful, we may find over time that we've become insensitive in other areas of our lives as well. All the time. On duty or off.

We no longer walk unguarded, unshielded, or accessible to others even for a moment. We've lost our wide-eyed innocence. And, sadly, our tender, sensitive side can be lost— seemingly forever.

But the truth is, we're not really impenetrable and insensitive. We're only protecting ourselves, and we don't know when or how to expose our deepest feelings in a way that isn't devastating. Like the porcupine, we curl up with our defensive mechanisms completely encircling what little inward tenderness we have left. And while such self-protection is understandable, it is counterproductive at best and totally self-sabotaging at worst.

You see, when the Lord speaks to us about letting down our guard and becoming vulnerable, He isn't expecting us to walk out into the unfriendly world wide open, weak, and helpless. He's not inviting us to go through life predisposed to all kinds of hazardous attack. No, His invitation is to come close to Him, trust Him enough to uncurl and expose our tender areas in His presence—but only to Him. To come to Him defenseless, uncovered, and exposed—in a word, *vulnerable . . . but only to Him.*

It's hard to make that transition, isn't it? It is for me. When my life has been fortified with safe escapes, emotional fences, and even a degree of callousness, it's hard to let down my guard—even with Him. Being distant and detached has become a habit of survival.

But when we allow such remoteness, do we realize that the price we pay is intimacy? How hard it is, when buffeted by criticism and stretched beyond our human limits, to come before the Lord and say, "Search me, O God." Scary, huh? "Know my heart; test me and know my anxious thoughts."

You can trust Him, remember? *The name of the LORD is a strong tower, the righteous run to it and are safe* (Proverbs

18:10). You can also depend on Him: *The eternal God is your refuge, and underneath are the everlasting arms* (Deuteronomy 33:27). Now, safe in the strong tower of His name, with His everlasting arms securely underneath, can you say, "Search me, O God, and know my heart"? Can you say, "See here, O Lord; here is where I've been wounded. And there is a scar I can't even admit is still there"? Can you trust God enough to say, "Test me, Lord; know my anxious thoughts," then spell them out to Him one by one?

————

When life takes more than it gives, how do you try to "balance the budget" emotionally, spiritually, and physically? In other words, what do you do to compensate?

If you were able to trust God enough to be totally vulnerable to Him, what self-defensive attitude or mannerism would you have to lay aside?

- skepticism
- sarcasm
- doubt
- fear
- callousness
- other

After you determine to be vulnerable to Him, what is the first thing you would like to say to Him?

If He were to test you and to know your anxious thoughts, what do you think they would be?

In a prayer, express to God what you need of Him now that you've chosen to open yourself and be vulnerable to Him. Write that prayer here:

Chapter
· 9 ·

Shelter From the Storm

Read Psalm 27.
Reflect on verse 5, a phrase at a time.

For in the day of trouble . . .

Is this going to last forever? Will this "day of trouble" ever be behind me? How many times have we cried out to God for an end to a certain difficult situation or crisis? Upon first reading of this passage, this little phrase can be passed over quickly by those of us who have endured not a day of trouble, but an unending season of it. If it's not one thing, it's another. We just "put out one fire" when another blazes to life. Long-term behavior problems in a child, illness of a spouse, uncertainty of the future—the list could go on and on. "It's wonderful that the Lord can deliver on any given day of trouble," we say. "But what about my situation? Is He good for the long haul?" The word "day" in this verse really means "reign," "time," or, "as long as." It means even when trouble, distress, and misery go on day after day, as long as the misery or disturbance continues "he will keep me safe in his dwelling." The promise is that there is a safe place for me to live, that God is in charge of my safekeeping.

He will hide me in the shelter of his tabernacle. . . .

No place to hide, no place to run to? Not for me. For me there is a safe place to tuck myself into and find refuge, retreat, and restoration—all while the storms of my life still rage about me. I can duck in out of the storm and know He will hide me in the shelter of His presence. I am a member of his household and have the key to the front door of His sanctuary where it is safe and secure. It is not necessarily a physical place, but it is a spiritual one.

. . . and set me high upon a rock.

Things look quite different from up here on the rock. When I was a child living in the Mojave Desert of southern California, I would often climb up on the large rock outcroppings that jutted from the mountain. Just a three- or four-foot-high ledge made the entire world look different to me. In reality it wasn't any different, but from that higher place I gained new perspective. I could see farther down into the valley below. Sometimes I even climbed up on the chicken coop. From there I could see still farther—almost forever. It's the same now. When I take the time out of my busy day and heavy responsibilities to get alone with God for just a few unguarded moments, He lifts me above the trials of my life and lets me see things from a different perspective. High up, emotionally and spiritually above the demands of my circumstances, I often marvel at how different everything looks from there.

No wonder David wrote verse six: "Then my head will be exalted above the enemies who surround me; at his tabernacle will I sacrifice with shouts of joy; I will sing and make music to the LORD."

Know this, weary Christian: God knows you are exposed to difficulty. He understands your perspective—He is aware of how you see the endless hardship you encounter. And He offers you shelter—today, right now, this very moment. He is faithfully, protectively offering you the shelter of His love. The hideaway of His presence and a new perspective from the tower of His strength.

But you will have to avail yourself of it. He's not going to grab you by the arm and drag you away. You'll have to scurry for shelter amid the pelting drops of your rainy-day life. Won't you seek His shelter from time to time? How about right now? Wouldn't this be a good time to begin?

What keeps you from slipping away from family and friends for a few moments each day, to be alone in God's presence on a regular basis?

If God were to beckon you into a momentary place of shelter, what excuse would you most likely give for putting it off until a later time?

Have you ever delayed, indefinitely postponed, or even canceled your quiet time?

For what reasons?

When in God's presence, are you now more likely to drop your guard than you were before you began reading this section? Why or why not?

Chapter
· 10 ·

Sustained by
His Mercy

Read Psalm 57:1.
Reflect further on 2 Samuel 24:14:

> *David said to Gad, "I am in deep distress. Let us fall into the hands of the LORD, for his mercy is great; but do not let me fall into the hands of men."*

If anyone knows the meaning of the words *endless, relentless,* and *nonstop,* it is my friend Claudia. She and her husband, Joe, are the parents of three children by birth, four by adoption, and numerous foster children. They are right at this moment anticipating the addition to their family of three little brothers. With two children in college, two in junior high, two in elementary school, and one in kindergarten, their household is busy, noisy, and the hub of activity. Claudia drives a twelve-passenger van like the rest of us drive our minivans.

"How do you do it?" she is often asked. Because we have such a close friendship, I have also asked her, "How do you survive?" Day after day, week after week, I stand in amazement as I observe her calm personality, patient demeanor, and her almost supernatural ability to stay on top of it all. Ongoing school and sports activities, frequent trips to the doctor and dentist, and around-the-clock duty ministering to her children would leave the rest of us gasping for air and groping for even a moment of privacy. But not her. Claudia is one of the most remarkable women I have ever met. And our lives, while running parallel in many ways, are so very different.

When I asked her, "How do you manage to stay within God's reach?" Claudia responded without hesitation. "Simple. I never let myself get beyond it." Would you like to know her technique, her strategy?

First, she says, "I maintain private worship almost continually. While I'm doing other things, I let my inner self reach toward God and worship Him. When I sense my attitudes lagging behind my intentions or my emotional energy drooping, I simply take a few minutes to hold still in a previously prepared inner place where I can tap back into God's strength and purpose for my life.

"I don't have a lot of physical *space* I can call my own, so I have to prepare an inner place—a place I call my safe place within the safe place (the home) I have created for my children.

"I also view corporate worship as more important than ever," she said. "How many times I have stood in the back of the church during worship holding a baby someone else has damaged through alcohol or drugs, and rocked that little one vigorously while letting the atmosphere of praise and worship surround both me and the baby."

When the emotionally and physically neglected or abused children placed in her home first arrive, Claudia takes them to church immediately to be immersed in the company of God's people in corporate worship. She says, "I keep in touch with healthy members of the body of Christ this way. Even if I must walk the halls of the church during worship with a fussy baby, I have to be there—for me!"

Claudia is a living example of James 5:10–11, which says, "Brothers, as an example of patience in the face of suffering, take the prophets who spoke in the name of the Lord. As you know, we consider blessed those who have persevered. You have heard of Job's perseverance and have seen what the Lord finally brought about. The Lord is full of compassion and mercy."

Claudia is not only an administrator of God's mercy to the children in her home, she ministers His mercy to me as well. When my husband and I were both ill for a few months, Claudia would arrive (on her way to some ball game or school drama performance), her van stuffed with children, and deliver home-cooked meals carefully prepared and frozen for us to pop in the oven and enjoy. I've seen her manage to find a few hours to be a part of a prayer team administering God's mercy to a hurting person. Motivated by mercy, she is an excellent example for all of us who need to learn how to let down our guard and avail ourselves of God's mercy.

More than Claudia loves her kids, God loves you and me. More than Claudia's seemingly boundless supply of energy, God's power is available to us. More than Claudia's around-the-clock availability to her children, God is available to you—to me. And more than the mercy that so graciously motivates Claudia, God is full of mercy—He *is* mercy.

Then, because we believe that, let us identify with David when he speaks to the prophet Gad and says, "I am in deep distress. Let us fall into the hands of the LORD, for his mercy is great" (2 Samuel 24:14). We can only let down our guard and successfully move on to the next phase of our study when we see God as totally merciful. Only then can we say wholeheartedly, "Have mercy on me, O God, have mercy on me, for in you my soul takes refuge. I will take refuge in the shadow of your wings until the disaster has passed" (Psalm 57:1).

————

Write out a dictionary definition of mercy here:

If you saw God as totally merciful, how would that change the way you approach Him?

How can you, like Claudia, prepare an inner place to return to for a touch of God's mercy when the going gets tough?

If you were to cry out to God for mercy, what specific situation would you be referring to?

How do you expect God to answer that cry?

Are you open to hear His voice?

What do you think He wants to say? Write it out here:

Section III

Open Your Heart

———

*A*nd I will bring you to the land I swore with uplifted hand to give to Abraham, to Isaac and to Jacob. I will give it to you as a possession. I am the LORD." Moses reported this to the Israelites, but they did not listen to him because of their discouragement and cruel bondage.

EXODUS 6:8–9

FOR MANY OF US whose lives seem to take much more than is returned, even a promise of God can seem unreal, and instead of welcoming it, we reject it. *Promises, promises,* we think. *I've heard all this before and nothing's changed.* The ropes of our circumstances can seem so tightly wound that we are hesitant to let God whisper anything of promise into our hearts. We can want His provision, His strength, or even His intervention, but be closed to His person—to Him.

In the last two sections of this book we covered two very important things to incorporate into our already overtaxed lives. But we can do those things—come into God's presence, even let down our guard—and still keep a shell around our hearts. Yes, it's true. We can long for His nearness, want to be secure and safe, but not be intimately open to Him. If that is what you do, you can learn to find ways to open to Him anew and to regain a precious closeness and intimacy in your relationship to Him. This section will show you how.

Chapter
• 11 •

After All I've Done for You!

Read 2 Chronicles 32:1–26.
Reflect also on Psalm 26:2:

Test me, O LORD, and try me, examine my heart and my mind.

"After all I've done for you!" We've all been tempted to say it now and then. "And you do this to me!" Even King Hezekiah might have been tempted to say it when he discovered that, after all he had done in obedience, the Lord was more than a little put out with him.

In 2 Chronicles, chapter 32, the story unfolds. Hezekiah had been a faithful king and steward of all God had entrusted to him, only to discover that he was being threatened by a king named Sennacherib, who was determined to make war on Jerusalem. But Hezekiah was a man of wisdom and held great persuasive powers to encourage his people. "Be strong and courageous," he told his men. "Do not be afraid or discouraged because of the king of Assyria and the vast army with him, for there is a greater power with us than with him" (v. 7).

Successful defensive strategies were put into place as Hezekiah proclaimed, "With him [Sennacherib] is only the arm of flesh, but with us is the LORD our God to help us and to fight our battles" (v. 8).

Of course, when Sennacherib heard about Hezekiah's

trust in God, he scoffed and even ridiculed not only Hezekiah, but God himself. He began to heckle the men stationed on Jerusalem's walls and caused no little disturbance, which drove not only Hezekiah, but Isaiah as well, to prayer. You can read for yourself what happened in detail, but the outcome of this battle was that Sennacherib hadn't counted on hand-to-hand combat with God's forces, which consisted of one lone angel who annihilated the aggressors!

In verse 22 of 2 Chronicles 32, it says that God saved Hezekiah and the people of Jerusalem not only from the hand of Sennacherib but from others as well. It says He took care of them on every side.

Even so, Hezekiah almost experienced a defeat beyond anything Sennacherib could have meted out. For after all his faithfulness, obedience, and trust in God, Hezekiah became proud. I can only imagine his inner dialogue.

"I did good," he could have said to himself. "I trusted God. What a wise and wonderful thing I did by obeying God. I've been so faithful—not many can say that, I'll tell you. Boy, God is sure lucky to have someone as faithful, obedient, and trusting as me to work with. Why, if it hadn't been for my faithfulness, obedience, and complete trust, not to mention my prayers, God wouldn't have even had the opportunity to defeat our enemies this way. Praise God—He surely did pull it off, thanks to me."

At that point, Hezekiah became ill almost to the point of death, and when he prayed, God answered and gave him a miraculous sign. But instead of responding with gratitude, Hezekiah took it for granted. He had become proud in his heart (vv. 24–25).

Only when Hezekiah repented—and all of Jerusalem with him—did God turn His wrath away from coming down hard and fast on the prideful nation and its king.

Now, you may be wondering what this has to do with opening your heart. Simply this: the lesson of Hezekiah makes several important points for those of us who experience life taking more than it gives back. We can be very aware of God's hands in our circumstances—and even thankful at the beginning—but then something begins to creep into our attitudes. Taking God for granted is a common malady many of us fall into occasionally. "Why shouldn't He answer this prayer?" we say. "After all, He's answered my prayers before." Eventually we can fall right into the same trap of thinking God's glory and power depends on our praying, not on His answering. We may not say it outright, but our thinking goes like this: *I was faithful in bringing this need to Him, therefore as much of the credit goes to me as to Him.* Do you know what gives birth to this attitude? Pride. And what makes a room for it to occupy? The heart.

Even while living under the protection of God, depending on Him and being vulnerable to Him, it is our heart that can do us in—not under the pressures of our circumstances, but under the hand of God.

So ask yourself, have you ever given yourself a pat on the back because you have *given* God room to work through your own faithfulness, prayer, and trust?

Is there pride lurking around somewhere in your heart? Not the kind of pride that says, "I can do this without help from anyone, not even God," but the more subtle kind of pride that says, "Thank God for doing this, but thank me for asking Him."

———

Think back over the last few months or years. Can you recall ever having this attitude?

What is the Lord speaking to you about right now? Take a moment to listen, then write what you hear in the space below:

What do you want to say to the Lord in response?

Isn't it time you opened your heart and let the Holy Spirit search for areas of self-reliance and pride? The next few chapters will help you do just that. How tragic it would be to abide in His presence, find a safe place to drop our guard, then close our hearts to what He wants to do in and through us.

Help us, O Lord, to not only open our lives to you, but our hearts as well. Amen.

Chapter
· *12* ·

Beyond the
Heart of the
Matter

Read Psalm 38:1–9.
Then reflect on verse 9:

> *All my longings lie open before you, O Lord; my sighing is*
> *not hidden from you.*

In glaring contrast to Hezekiah, David rips open his inner self, exposing his gut-level feelings and raw soul completely to the Lord. Hezekiah harbored a tiny bit of pride inside until it had leavened his entire heart. David spews out his inner self, leaving his heart hollow, hungry for God. Hezekiah's attitudes revealed how he took God's graciousness for granted. David, on the other hand, drops his defenses, dumps out his passion, and pours out his soul. David literally clutches at God in prayer. Grasping hold of the reality of his sinful self and desperate need, he throws himself at God's feet, boldly admits his need for love and mercy, and hangs on for dear life.

Another interesting comparison of Hezekiah and David is this: what Hezekiah considered monumental (the approaching threat of his enemy), God saw as incidental. But what Hezekiah defined as incidental (the pride in his heart), God termed monumental. Hezekiah's life had been nearly exemplary; David's had been far from it. David had sinned, fallen away so far from God's plan that it seemed impossible to ever get back. He was pursued by his enemies and lived like anything but an anointed king. Yet David was considered the one "after God's own heart."

The point of this discussion is simply this: *It matters more to God what is in one's heart than what is in one's past.* Faithfulness does not eradicate pride any more than one's sin eradicates God's mercy and forgiveness. The lesson here is that God is more interested in the sum and substance of our lives than He is in our performance. What lies at the core of our inner self—our very essence—is what God is wanting to touch. You see, He not only wants to get to the heart of what matters to us, but to the *very heart of us*.

Aha, the nitty-gritty. Exactly. And what's more, if He is ever to get in touch with the real, true, and fundamental me, it will be because I have invited Him there.

In Psalm 38, we see David in touch first with his sinfulness, then his feelings, then his need. Only after all that was he able to get in touch with God about those areas.

We see David in remorse and in rejoicing. We ache with his repentance, celebrate with his praise. Let's learn from him as he shows us the importance of getting in touch not only with the heart of the matter, but with our own heart. Are we as courageous as David? Can you and I openheartedly invite God to the very core of our personality and existence?

Which of David's needs listed in Psalm 38:1–4 do you identify with?

Which of the needs in verses 5–8 sound familiar to you?

Now read verse 9. What longings would you like to lay open before the Lord?

What are the "sighings" you would like exposed to His love and care?

What do you fear about being totally open with God and pouring out your need as David did in this passage?

Chapter
· 13 ·

The Accessible Heart

Read Ephesians 3:16–19.
Reflect on these words from Psalm 139:23–24:

*Search me, O God, and know my heart; test me and know
my anxious thoughts. See if there is any offensive way in me,
and lead me in the way everlasting.*

An open heart is an accessible heart. "Yeah, sure," we
say. "I knew that."

But knowing it conceptually is one thing. Laying it wide
open and completely accessible is another.

As children, many of us learned to quote from memory
Revelation 3:20: "Behold, I stand at the door and knock: if
any man hear my voice, and open the door, I will come
in . . ." (KJV). God does not force entry into our lives or into
our hearts. He only occupies where He is allowed accessibility. Patiently He stands and knocks at the outer door of
our hearts until we give Him entry. At that moment when
we ask Him to come into our hearts and lives, He gladly enters and we begin this wonderful adventure of fellowship
with God through His Son and our Savior Jesus Christ.

The Bible uses the simple illustration of someone knock-
ing at the door of someone's house. We are taught to think
of it this way: Jesus comes to the doorstep of our heart. There
He stands and knocks gently until the door is opened and
He is invited in. Let's carry it a step further. Think of Him

as standing in your living room with visible access to other doorways to other rooms. Is He in your house? Yes. Is He in your heart and life? Yes. But as in your physical house, does He only have access to the living room—the place where you put on your best behavior—but not to your private self?

Some may have difficulty with the concept of a compartmentalized heart. When we invite Jesus in, they say, "He's in to stay." But does He have *access* to your entire heart once He's inside? Even David prayed to God for an *undivided* heart. "Teach me your way, O LORD, and I will walk in your truth; give me an undivided heart, that I may fear your name" (Psalm 86:11). Did he discover a division in his own heart? "I will praise you, O Lord my God, with all my heart" (Psalm 86:12). David had discovered the danger of trying to serve God with less than his whole heart.

If we are ever to live in triumph when life takes more than it returns to us, it will be because we have given God access to our entire heart-house. Hezekiah held back an area of his heart and filled it with pride. David held nothing back but humbly invited God to invade his entire self, and God filled him with joy and peace.

It is your choice. Just as Jesus stood at the outer door of your heart without forcing entry, He now inquires about the inner chambers. Are you willing to allow Him full access to the "closed-from-public-view" rooms of your heart?

In the list of comparative words below, check which best describe God's accessibility to the inner chambers of your heart:

- closed
- unclosed
- shut
- wide open
- secured
- gaping open
- locked
- enterable
- safely shut

70

- open and exposed to God's view
- out of sight or inquiry
- kept at arm's length
- within God's reach

Hezekiah kept a small room where he stored his pride. You may not have the problem with pride that this king did, but do you have rooms in your heart where you hide the following?

- personal emotional pain or trauma
- areas of unbelief or doubt
- futility and frustration with unanswered prayers
- mistrust of God and others
- unforgiveness
- unconfessed sin or works of the flesh
- disappointment
- personal desires, dreams, or secret ambitions
- other

If you were to say with David, "Search me, O God, and know my heart," what doors would you have to unlock?

What heart-stored secret places would you have to expose and open to God's view?

In all honesty, can you say you have a heart that is totally accessible to God?

Chapter · 14 ·

The Available Heart

Read John 14:15–23.
Reflect on verse 23:

> *Jesus replied, "If anyone loves me, he will obey my teaching. My Father will love him, and we will come to him and make our home with him."*

"Come on in," we say to our visitors. "Make yourselves at home." It's a figure of speech. We really don't expect them to do exactly that. Guests are waited on. Their desires are to be anticipated by their hosts. More coffee, more food, something cold to drink. Residents are expected to help themselves. Guests are not expected to do the laundry, take out the trash, or help with the housework. Quite a different story for those who live in the home.

In the last chapter, we invited Christ from the doorstep of our heart-home to the inside. Then we granted Him access to all the interior rooms and cubbyholes. But if we open our heart to Him, we must also extend the further invitation to make himself at home. To go from being a guest to being a resident. We are not giving Him access to our inner self—we are making our inner self *available* to Him as well.

Think of it in this way: I can go to the library, walk in, sit down, and read the daily paper. But in doing so I haven't really availed myself of all the services the library offers. Having *access* to the building isn't the same as having *access* to all the varied resources of the library. One library I love to visit in Redlands, California, has a heritage room. I have to make an appointment to go in there and look at the historical documents, old newspapers, and vintage maps of the community. But the librarian who is assigned to that division doesn't need an appointment—she has a key. She goes in and out at will. I have limited access; she has total availability. I'm the guest; she's the resident.

That's the kind of *homemaking* Jesus speaks about in John 14. For God to make His home in our hearts and lives, He has to have not only the front door key, but the keys to all the locked, inaccessible places. It means He comes and goes at will. Nothing is reserved, hidden, or concealed from Him. And then the adjustment begins.

Roommates, newlyweds, and other adults living away from home for the first time begin to understand that deciding to live with another person doesn't mean you'll be instantly at home with that person. Personal habits, eating and sleeping routines, and entertainment choices are only some of the issues that surface in a relationship that seemed to be blissfully perfect before cohabitation began. Suddenly nothing works except being candid and frank about even petty issues. Straightforward, honest communication has to be tempered with patience, tolerance, and love. Dwelling side by side, sharing the same house, kitchen, and closets forces us to drop pretenses and get down to the nitty-gritty of our personalities and pet peeves. It's where, as we say, "the rubber meets the road."

So too in our relationship with God. When we invite Him not only to come in, but to make himself at home, we are entering an entirely new dimension of openness, frankness, and boldness in our relationship with Him. This is when we take Him out of the church and into our homes. Out of the prayer closet and into the workplace. And it's where God begins to *interfere* with our deepest heartfelt issues. It's where He begins to interact with our prejudices, probe at our hidden agendas, and search out our secret desires.

Have you ever been cleaning the garage or storage area with your spouse and had him hold up something you've had tucked away and ask, "What in the world are you hanging on to this for?" Your defensive mechanisms whirl to life and you retort, "It's mine. I'll take care of it."

Have you had a similar experience with the indwelling Holy Spirit? Once He makes His home in your heart, He may whisper in your quiet time: "How about this attitude?" Then, "Why haven't you paid more attention to this bit of unforgiveness tucked away over there?"

It's risky to open your heart wide to invite Christ in, and then extend the invitation to include making himself at home. Yet do you really want less than a full relationship with Him?

When life takes more than it gives, do we really want to hide our emptiness, loneliness, and helplessness from Him any longer? Do we really want to continue to harbor those grudges, shelter our anger, or store our hopelessness indefinitely?

When my twenty-four-year-old son came home to finish his ministerial training, I had to go into the spare room, empty the closets, and sort through stuff that I hadn't had to deal with earlier because I didn't need the space. I had to throw away some things, give away some things, and find additional storage space for the rest. It's the same when God moves in.

Don't expect to accommodate God without some housecleaning taking place. You can't just move things around a bit and move others aside until He gets settled. When we invite God to make himself at home with us, we soon discover He takes more and more room in our heart-houses as time goes by. Eventually the entire place will be filled with His presence. What a wonderful thought!

———

Are you ready to invite God to "make himself at home" within your entire heart?

What are the areas that you'd like to keep off limits to Him?

If He were to shine His light into the deepest, darkest cubbyholes of your heart and life, what would you be tempted to hide from sight first?

If you were to ask God to come into your heart—in keeping with John 14:23—what would you say?

Write such a prayer here:

Can you do it? Can you say to God, "Come on in, make yourself at home"?

Chapter · 15 ·

The Teachable Heart

Read Psalm 143.
Underline in your Bible and reflect on these phrases from verses 8 and 10:

> *Bring me word of your unfailing love. . . . Show me the way I should go. . . . Teach me to do your will . . . lead me on level ground.*

Can you imagine giving birth to a baby, then never expecting that baby to grow, learn anything, or change? Of course not! It would be a terrible tragedy for a baby to remain a baby. So why would anyone enter into God's kingdom with no expectation of growth or learning? As new Christians, we certainly entertain no such thoughts. Like a baby learning to sit up, crawl, and walk, we can't wait to "get on with it," to learn all the exciting things God has for us. Yet somewhere along the way, when our daily responsibilities have weighed us down, and the burdens of life have discouraged us, we stop being excited about learning. We may even shrink back from God's presence and keep those inner recesses of our lives to ourselves—those inner chambers that God longs to enter and feel at home in. Perhaps we've allowed Him access to our heart-home, even made every room available for Him to enter at any time—yet we still shrink from letting Him go too far, allowing Him to *change* us, mold us into the image of His Son.

Lest we stop short of the entire dynamic of opening our hearts completely to the Father, let's examine the words of Psalm 143 and apply them to our lives.

Talk to me. . . .

Above all else, the Lord wants us to know and believe how much He loves us. It is the one thing He wants you to know today, more than anything you could ever imagine or hope for—the depth of His love and care for you. Right now, right here—in your immediate circumstance—He loves you.

Show me. . . .

In the safety and security of His love, He longs to show you His ways. Maybe the way you've been taking lately isn't working. The feelings you have been struggling with have overwhelmed you, and you know your ways are not His ways. Today, embraced by His love, ask Him to show you His path through the maze of your life.

Now let's picture our lives completely open to Him. Having given Him *access* to our heart, then making every room of our heart-home *available* to Him, we no longer restrict God when He moves through the corridors of our feelings, dreams, and disappointments. Nothing is concealed from His loving gaze, nothing hidden from His probing mercy. Transparent through and through we are ready to see ourselves and our situations with new eyes . . . with the perspective only He can give us.

Teach me. . . .

An open heart is a teachable heart. Touched by God's love and insight into our circumstances, now we can, with full assurance and confidence, whisper the most desperate, heart-humble prayer of all: "Teach me, Lord." With our innermost selves laid bare and exposed to the love and mercy of God, we drop our defenses, pour out our souls, and grasp onto our living Lord for instruction: "Don't just *show* me a better way, *teach* me to do it!"

Lead me. . . .

Take me by the hand, Father is our heart's prayer. *Walk me through this.* Once we are teachable, we are trainable. In fact,

78

we are changeable. Yes, it's true. Though we may be scarred and disillusioned, we are still changeable. We are not stuck in bitterness, failure, and disappointment forever. We are openhearted before a loving and understanding God. He knows our weaknesses; He knows our stress points. He knows our needs, and has a better understanding of our responsibilities than we do. What's more, He can not only change our circumstances, he can change *us!* Sometimes He prefers to do just that, while leaving the circumstances as they are . . . and for good reason: Changing us is often the key to changing our circumstances.

Let me illustrate. Once I was in the hospital, very ill and in a great deal of pain. The hours seemed to drag on endlessly while nurses, dear friends, and family members tried everything they knew to make me comfortable. Prayers for healing seemed to go unheard. For days I suffered, and unless God performed a miracle, I thought, there would be no change for the better.

Finally exhausted, I stopped struggling against the pain and discomfort. Crying out to God didn't seem to do any good; I had to try something else. Although it went against my nature, and even my Christian beliefs, I finally gave up— first to God, then to the pain. I embraced only Him—not His answer, not His miracle, only Him. I gave up hoping for change and hoped only in the Lord.

Then an interesting thing happened. A different nurse took charge of my case, someone with another perspective, perhaps more experience. She came into my room, took one look at me, and left again without a word, returning a few moments later with the *exact thing* I needed to relieve my discomfort. Someone who saw the whole situation with new understanding made all the difference. Did my circumstances change? Not much. I was still very sick, and my recovery would be long and tedious. But God changed me in the midst of my circumstances. My attitude changed, and that started me down the road toward healing in His way and in His time. When I finally rested in Him and accepted my situation, He brought about a most unexpected and simple solution to the immediate problem. That one minor change of approach in my care became a turning point. I was able to rest for several hours and God began to heal me in His own way.

Your circumstances can change too, as *you* change. Very often, it is the change in your own heart that opens the door for God to bring change into your circumstances.

———————

Since you started this study, have your circumstances changed much?

Have they gotten worse? If so, how?

How have *you* changed since the beginning of this study?

Are you more apt to be openhearted now?

What are you doing to keep your heart open?

Comment on this statement: *If God is to get to the heart of the matter, He must first get to the heart of me.*

How are you applying that to your life?

If God were to bring a change into your circumstances from a change deep from within you, how do you think He would do that? Where would He begin?

Section IV

Let God Love You

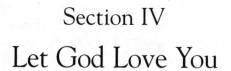

My command is this: Love each other as I have loved you. Greater love has no one than this, that he lay down his life for his friends.

JOHN 15:12–13

IN LAYING DOWN our lives for those who depend on us for care, we often forget how much God loves *us*. Feeling overburdened, with no end in sight to the pressure in our lives, we can feel empty and spent. And if we don't take the time to understand the concept of God's love for us, we can feel used and burned out. The demands of caring for others can frequently prevent us from taking the time to reconnect with the fact that God loves us—more than we love Him, more than we love those in our care.

Perhaps you were hesitant to come into His presence, let down your guard, and open your heart. You were afraid to be vulnerable, fearful of more responsibility added to your already impossible list. But I am living proof that God will never seduce you into a place of intimacy and then destroy your inner self. He will never smooth talk His way into your heart and then manipulate you into doing things for Him.

Here's a challenge: For the next five days, let God love you. Just the way you are. Even if you're sour on church, your home, or your work. Even if you're disillusioned with being a Christian, bound by responsibilities you believe God has required of you. Set all that aside and let Him love you. Nothing more.

Let Him love you without regard to your failures, your successes, your performance, or your lack of it. God waits to pour out His love on you.

Chapter
· 16 ·

Love Without
Measure

Read Psalm 147:1–11.
Reflect on verses 10–11:

His pleasure is not in the strength of the horse, nor his delight in the legs of a man; the LORD delights in those who fear him, who put their hope in his unfailing love.

I watched Todd with admiration. The divorce was devastating, and he ached not only for his failed marriage but for his children. When he became a Christian, his wife simply bailed out. Dating during the late sixties and married in the early seventies, their relationship was based on rebelling against society and easing their maladjustment through drugs, alcohol, and "free love." Empty and barren in spirit, Todd searched further. He explored Eastern mysticism before running into a street evangelist who led him to Christ and directed him to a Bible-believing coffeehouse-type ministry, which later guided him to a church. His wife didn't join him, and eventually gave him the ultimatum: "Jesus or me."

I met Todd at that low point in his life. Not only did he have to choose between his wife and Jesus, but the choice was made more difficult by the fact that they had a child, with another on the way. His wife made it perfectly clear that she didn't want a Christian husband. She preferred the life they used to have—a life Todd knew he would have to leave behind.

Staying faithful to Christ wasn't easy at such a price, but through dark days and periods of deep loneliness Todd never turned back to the old ways. He'd become a Christian, and he was going to remain faithful no matter what the cost.

My friend learned the dynamic of living at a level of commitment to Christ that appeared to take much more than it gave. I'd like to be able to tell you that his wife eventually saw the change in him, was drawn to the Lord, and they were reunited. But it didn't happen. My friend stood by and watched his wife spend her precious youth on drugs and one failed relationship after another. He maintained open communication with her and fulfilled his responsibility to his children, eventually enrolling them in a Christian school. I could hardly believe it when I learned that every morning he went to her house, fed and dressed the children while she slept, then drove them to school. He worked straight through his lunch hour so he could take an hour at the end of their school day to pick them up and take them home again.

You can only imagine that such commitment gave him little time for a social life of his own. But he often said that his own needs were met in meeting those of his children.

"How do you do it?" I asked him.

"I've learned to depend on God's love," he answered. "The minute I begin to think of the strength I need, or the patience, or the constant forgiveness that is required to maintain this kind of lifestyle, I begin to falter and get angry. But when I depend on God's love, I find the inner strength I need, not only to cope, but to continue, even though there is no end in sight."

Even God must be impressed with this young man's resolve and commitment, I thought to myself. Not so. Our Psalm 147 passages tells us this.

Often we make the mistake of assuming, ever so subtly, that God is bound to notice the great strength and endurance with which we face the emotionally difficult situations in our lives. But God isn't impressed with the clever use of our resources, nor with our superwoman emotional attitudes. God is impressed with one thing—our dependence on His love. He doesn't take pleasure in self-sufficient, self-reliant martyrs who face their challenging situations head on with self-confidence and self-made wills of iron. He delights in those who throw themselves day after day on the inexhaustible riches of His merciful love.

Then, on those days when there is no hope, no way out, and no end to the difficulty of the circumstance, there is still His love. When there is no strength left, no answers to be found, there is His love. A resource of strength that can't be measured, confined, or limited by our daily challenges. His love is there, readily available and free for the asking.

Do you want to delight the Father today? Depend on His love—and nothing else.

———

In what ways do you easily slip into depending on your own strength, ingenuity, or resourcefulness to handle your challenging responsibilities?

What signals—or reminders—would trigger you to realize when you've stopped depending on His love and are depending on yourself?

How do you think your life would change if you depended more on Him and less on yourself?

In the form of a prayer, write out your own "Declaration of Dependence."

Chapter · 17 ·

Nurturing the Seed of God's Love

Read 1 John 4:7–16.
Reflect on verses 9–10, then again on these words from verse 10:

> *This is love: not that we loved God, but that he loved us.* . . .

Every Christian writer I know understands the danger and risk of lifting a phrase out of a passage of Scripture. Yet sometimes we swallow such large quantities of God's Word in our effort to understand complete and whole concepts and principles, we can overlook nuggets of life-changing truth. To be true to Scripture and to point out small treasures of truth at the same time is best left to biblical scholars, which I am not. Yet this phrase, "Not that we loved God, but that he loved us . . ." is worth a pause in our Scripture reading. A pause, not to lift it from its context and give it our own meaning or interpretation, but to meditate on its implications for a deeper understanding of God's love.

I'm reminded of a walk through one of the giant redwood groves in Yosemite National Park near my home. One is tempted to walk among those overwhelming trees with your neck craned and eyes straining toward the painful brightness of the blue sky. The bigness of the giant sequoias assaults the senses. The brain can't quite interpret the size of trunks and branches and begins to ache trying to shrink the image of the stately cedars into a known frame of reference. But one day I just shut my eyes and tried to absorb the silence of the oversized forest. In reverence, not for the trees but for their Creator, I bowed my head prayerfully. When I opened my eyes, there at my feet lay the tiniest of pine cones, barely the size of a pullet egg—smaller than the smallest hen egg commercially available. The pine cone of the giant redwood is easily overlooked. Yet from that small cone, there is potential for thousands of seedlings. At that stage, one human being can hold hundreds of these giant trees in the palm of his hand. Yet, at maturity, eight grown men holding hands cannot stretch themselves enough to encircle the trunk of some of these magnificent trees.

The entire fourth chapter of 1 John relates our ability to love others with our personal experience and understanding of God's love. To walk through it as a whole is tantamount to a stroll among the giant redwoods. Awesome, yet overwhelming. Let me explain.

Current and popular psychological teaching says that unless we love ourselves, we cannot genuinely love others. I disagree. I believe that unless we've experienced for ourselves God's immeasurable love, we cannot love others.

Sadly, many Christians do not carry a consciousness of God's deep and abiding love. They only catch glimpses of it from time to time. They may even feel it at varying degrees of intensity, depending on the atmosphere of corporate worship or fellowship. But to abide in it continually is, tragically, a rare experience for many—if not most. Even those occupied in God's work full time have to be reminded that while their service may be an expression of their love for God—it began with His love for them.

Then, in our experience with Christ and the exploration of His Word, we come across a chapter like 1 John 4. Wow! "No wonder I'm not feeling God's love more," we tell ourselves. "I need to love others more." But, in reality, the opposite is true. We don't love others more because we need to know more of God's love.

So we pause at this phrase, lifted from Scripture, but not out of context: "not that we loved God, but that He loved us." In fact, this tiny seedling of a giant truth, when placed in the context of our experience and understanding of the way God looks at our love relationship with Him, puts the entire context of 1 John 4 deep within our spirits—to germinate and produce first the sapling, then the adolescent tree on its way to becoming one of the giant redwoods in His kingdom.

Have I tried to love others without experiencing God's love for me first?

Have I tried to love God as if I were the initiator of the relationship, rather than recognizing that His love reached out to me long before I reached out to Him?

How does this concept, *not that I love God, but that He loves me,* change how you receive God's love?

If you and I were sitting across the room from each other, and I said, "Let God love you," how would you respond in light of 1 John 4:10?

Write a note to God telling Him that you receive His love, and how you receive it. Close your note with words expressing your love for Him.

Chapter
· 18 ·

God's
Reaching Love

Read Romans 5:1–8.
Reflect on verses 5–8:

> *And hope does not disappoint us, because God has poured out his love into our hearts by the Holy Spirit, whom he has given us. You see, at just the right time, when we were still powerless, Christ died for the ungodly. Very rarely will anyone die for a righteous man, though for a good man someone might possibly dare to die. But God demonstrates his own love for us in this: While we were still sinners, Christ died for us.*

It's easy to understand loving the worthy, the well-behaved, the deserving. We do it all the time. We bribe our children, reward our friends, and, in fact, expect the same in return. Why? Because we want others to behave or perform in more acceptable and pleasing ways—to make them more "lovable." No wonder it's so difficult to grasp a loving, forgiving God who loved us at His best when we were at our worst. Only God truly loves the unlovable.

Each of us has experienced the gap between what we perceive we should be, or even want to be, and what we really are. It's what I call the "Gotta Be's" or the "Wanna Be's" versus the "Is's."

We know we should be more grateful, more patient, more thankful, more loving, more tolerant—the list is endless. We also know that if we were in charge, we wouldn't tolerate some of the secret attitudes we harbor in our own hearts. But we are not in charge—God is. Good thing, don't you agree?

If God waited until we were at our very best before He loved us, we'd be in a sorry state indeed. God loves—period. No conditions, no prerequisites. Nothing except that we acknowledge our need of His love and are willing to accept it. No attempt at earning it will be rewarded; there is no way to buy it or to perform our way into His good graces.

God is love, the Bible says in 1 John 4. And yet . . .

I have titled this section "Let God Love You," and yet the Bible clearly teaches that He is the initiator of this love, not us. How then can we *let* Him love us? Can we stop Him?

Once one of my teenagers was struggling with life in general and with me in particular. One day I simply realized that while she might be able to stop me from expressing my love directly, she could not stop me from loving her. What joy, however, when the season of estrangement came to an end and once again she let me express my love for her in a more direct and tangible way. So it is with God. We can't stop Him from loving us. Romans 5:8 makes that perfectly clear. But we can shut off His love from directly and intimately reaching us . . . touching us.

So, the challenge—let God love you. Let His love reach you and touch you in those places where there is a gap between what you ought to be, or want to be, and what you really are.

Falling short of your present responsibilities? Let God love you there. Impatient with those with whom you need to be more loving and merciful? Let God love you there. Angry with those who have done you harm? Let God love you there. And when life takes more than it gives—let God love you there, too.

You see, a love that flowed even when we were sinners and outcasts from God's family certainly can flow now when we're just weary, tired, or coming up short. But as my teenage daughter did to me, I too have cut off the personally experienced expression of God's love more than once in my lifetime. And when I'm living with what I perceive to be an emotional deficit—considering what I'm required to give out compared to what I take in—I've learned to let God love me there. Yes, right there where it hurts the most. And so can you.

Before answering today's questions, think first of three or four of your close relationships where you are required to give more than you receive.

Now, for the next twenty minutes or so, in prayer envision yourself grasping hold of a measure of God's love and applying it to those situations. Extend your hand upward, holding it before God with this in mind. Then close it around a portion of His love. Now physically open your hand and touch your forehead or chest, and ask Him to touch that deficit situation with His love. In this tangible way, let God touch you with His love.

———————

If you let God love you where you are coming up short, where you're giving more than you're getting, how would that change you?

How would it change your situation?

How would it change the way you see or handle your situation?

Chapter
· 19 ·

An Endless Reservoir of Love

Read John 3:16 several times.
Reflect on the following phrase:

For God so loved the world that he gave his one and only Son.

It can become so familiar that we miss its beauty and the eternal significance of these wonderful words most of us memorized as children. Words that lie at the very foundation of our faith in Jesus Christ as our personal Savior can lose their impact and meaning to our everyday life. Once we've accepted Christ we tend not to revisit these words. How sad. For in them lies the truth of why it's so important to let God love us. He also knows what it's like to give beyond reason. To have someone (you and me, for example) need something only He can give, when it will cost Him dearly. And He knows what it's like to love at such a level that no sacrifice, no price, is too high to pay for the reward of what it will bring.

Furthermore, He paid this price in order that you and I would be able to receive not only His Son but His love.

Once again, God's expression of love proves that He isn't like us. There is simply no way to reduce to human level the love behind salvation's plan. God's love isn't a stifled, bottled-up kind of love. It begs, searches, and seeks avenues of expression that you and I might receive it. God doesn't feel love—He gives it. It's not His emotion—it is Him!

God loved and then God gave.

We often do just the opposite. Many times we give, and then because of the personal investment in the object of our action, we begin to love. We treasure the things that have cost us much, but God treasures first, then pays the price.

If you and I were sitting across the table from each other sharing a quiet cup of tea and private conversation, I would want you to know how much God loves you. How much He longs for you to first believe, then receive. Not because of what you have or haven't done. Not because of who you are or aren't. God loves you. Simple, straightforward, no ifs, ands, or buts. He loves you.

And, what's more, He always has. He loved you long before you were born. Before the Declaration of Independence was signed or the Constitution was drafted. He loved you before Columbus set sail from Spain or before Stephen was stoned to death. Before Jesus called the disciples from their nets to follow Him or before Paul was blinded on the road to Damascus. He loved you before David danced in victory or ran from Saul. He loved you before Abraham and Isaac, before Moses—yes, even before Adam. He has loved you from before the beginning of time and will love you long after it ceases.

In this one minute sliver of eternity, won't you take hold of that eternal, undeniable love and let it carry you through today? Won't you dare to believe that the love that could make a difference in the eternal destiny of humankind can make a difference in your life this afternoon?

Don't look to the others around you to supply your ever-increasing need for love and acceptance. Look to God. Look to His Son and your Savior Jesus Christ. This is where your endless reservoir of love is found. Your circumstances may squeeze the life out of you—Jesus can put it back. Your responsibilities may weigh you down and give you nothing in return, but Jesus lightens your load by carrying not only it—but you, as well.

God hasn't given you this pathway to prove your love for Him . . . but to prove His love for you. He can meet you here, right here where life is at its toughest and roughest. He can love you even in the middle of your present and never-ceasing struggle. Will you let Him?

―――――――

In what ways do you think you could be stifling, or have stifled in the past, God's expression of love for you?

How can you make sure that you'll let Him love you?

Recall the last time you sensed God's perfect love superseding your own imperfect love for Him and others.

What prayer do you think would be appropriate to pray right now? Write it here.

Chapter · 20 ·

A New Perspective

Read Pslam 25.
Reflect on Psalm 13:5:

> *But I trust in your unfailing love; my heart rejoices in your salvation.*

As I write this, I am standing up—a strange and unfamiliar position for me to write in, but a recently pulled muscle makes it necessary. I don't tell you this for your sympathy, for when you finally read this I will be healed and the temporary discomfort long forgotten. However, it serves as an illustration of our focus on God's love these past days.

Here at my makeshift workstation, nothing is as handy, things get lost more easily, and I don't seem to be as coordinated as when I'm in my usual, familiar position. Yet despite the inconvenience, I'm enjoying being able to easily pace the floor when I want to think ... to stretch when I feel my muscles getting tired. And, what's more, my desk looks entirely different when I'm standing rather than sitting down in my chair. This new, if somewhat awkward, standing position gives me an entirely new perspective while I'm working. I can see farther out the window; I can move about the room and change my position more easily. Sure it feels strange to reach down to answer the phone, but then I can comfortably step back from my keyboard as I talk. Much more easily, in fact, than if I were sitting.

That's the same feeling I get when I remember to take the time from the demands of my day and family to let God love me . . . to let Him move me to another level and give me His perspective of my workload and those who need me. It's awkward at first, just like it is for you. But then, after a while I begin to discover the other benefits of a new perspective. I am more apt to see into the distance, instead of just coping with the demands of the moment. God's love experienced over and over helps me maneuver more easily, and I am better able to remain on my feet rather than be blindsided and knocked for an emotional loop by my heavy responsibilities. I am simply more spiritually mobile and fit when I let God shower upon me the marvelous reality of His unfailing love.

Remembering to let Him love me helps me gain distance when necessary, and to risk closeness when needed. It helps minimize my weariness, and maximize my effectiveness. It fills my emptiness . . . comforts me when I'm lonely. God's unchanging, immeasurable love fortifies me with strength, and yet softens me with compassion.

In other words, when I let God love me, I discover I grow more like Him toward those who need me to love them. It helps me see that my life isn't more give than take, especially when I can take all I need from Him. When life takes more than it gives, God's love can give back much more than you and I will ever need. His love more than balances any emotional deficit we can experience.

How about you? Need more patience, love, forgiveness, tolerance, and compassion? Then let Him love you. Are you coming up short in attitude or commitment toward those who demand so much from you day in and day out? Let God love you.

Then, over and over, let Him love you again and again.

———————

How has this simple concept changed how you view God's love for you?

How has it helped you see your need of His love differently?

How does letting God love you change how you see those who need you differently?

Now, safe in the arms of your loving heavenly Father, snuggle close and listen—He has something He wants to say. In fact, there are several things I think He wants to say. That's what the next section is about: hearing His voice as you experience His perfect love.

Section V

Listen to His Voice

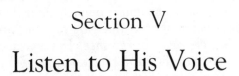

Come, let us bow down in worship, let us kneel before the LORD our Maker; for he is our God and we are the people of his pasture, the flock under his care. Today, if you hear his voice, do not harden your hearts.

PSALM 95:6–8

I TELL YOU THE TRUTH, the man who does not enter the sheep pen by the gate, but climbs in by some other way, is a thief and a robber. The man who enters by the gate is the shepherd of his sheep. The watchman opens the gate for him, and the sheep listen to his voice. He calls his own sheep by name and leads them out. When he has brought out all his own, he goes on ahead of them, and his sheep follow him because they know his voice. But they will never follow a stranger; in fact, they will run away from him because they do not recognize a stranger's voice (John 10: 1–5).

Do we really believe God's Word? Can we actually accept as fact the concept that God desires to speak to and with His people as He has from the beginning? Can you accept the idea that God has something to say to you?

For the next five days, listen—not to the voice of a stranger, but to the voice of God himself. He's got some wonderful things He'd like to say to you.

Chapter · 21 ·

The Voice That Refreshes

Read John 4:4–26 and John 10:1–5.
Reflect on these words from verses 25 and 26:

> The woman said, "I know that Messiah" (called Christ) "is coming. When he comes, he will explain everything to us." Then Jesus declared, "I who speak to you am he."

> I tell you the truth, the man who does not enter the sheep pen by the gate, but climbs in by some other way, is a thief and a robber. The man who enters by the gate is the shepherd of his sheep. The watchman opens the gate for him, and the sheep listen to his voice. He calls his own sheep by name and leads them out. When he has brought out all his own, he goes on ahead of them, and his sheep follow him because they know his voice. But they will never follow a stranger; in fact, they will run away from him because they do not recognize a stranger's voice.

Nothing is quite as uncomfortable as being an outsider. Left out of society, excluded from the usual community activities where other women gathered each morning and evening, a Samaritan woman slips to the well in the middle of the day. Perhaps it was too painful to be ignored or even openly shunned by the others—it was better to go alone when she could be sure she'd endure no more pain. Playing it safe. A woman of shadowed reputation, she may even have thought she deserved exclusion or embarrassment.

No matter what her past, Jesus addressed her openly, honestly, and without hesitancy. I wonder, given her previous experience with men, if she suspected that Jesus was just another man interested in her for less than honorable reasons.

"Just give me a drink of water," was His simple, but remarkable, request. "Share with me some of what you have."

Can you imagine how she must have felt? Could she really believe that was all He wanted? He a Jew, and she a lowly Samaritan? Even societal prejudice would exclude her.

"Excuse me?" she seems to be saying. "Are you aware of the cultural differences between us? And you ask me to give you a drink?"

In His answer, "If you knew the gift of God and who it is that asks you . . ." Jesus reveals that He is much more than a Jew. And suddenly the cultural barriers fall, and the differences between righteousness and sin, as well as life and death, become obvious. Yet Jesus often taught against judgmentalism. But how was she to know? She hadn't heard Him—she had only heard about Him, yet all the while unaware of the fact that this *was Him* speaking to her at that moment.

Yes, right there in the middle of her situation, in spite of her lower-than-low status, Jesus spoke to her. He came into her world, into her town, and invited her to give Him a drink of well water. Then He spoke to her about a living water that she needed more than He could possibly need the cool, clear liquid in her container. When Jesus spoke to her that hot, dusty afternoon, nothing would ever be the same again. All of a sudden, unexpectedly, her life forever changed.

And it's the same for you—and thankfully for me, too.

Here in the routine, even the drudgery of our lives, Jesus appears. Not in some ethereal way reminiscent of hallucination—but in a real, tangible speaking way. In these moments, as we slip away from our routine to draw from the well of our daily devotional life, He speaks to us from His Word. And, like the woman at the well, we too often question His motives and even His methods.

"I know," we say, "that Jesus is coming. That I will see

Him move in my situation and change my circumstance—
someday."

I tell you, my friend, Jesus is here. This is the day. He
comes to us. He goes out of His way so we don't have to go
out of ours. He meets us right here, in the middle of our pain,
in the center of our loneliness, and within the circle of our
responsibilities. And He speaks to us the same comforting
words He spoke to the Samaritan woman: "I who speak to
you am he."

Think of all the things that might have been spoken to
the Samaritan woman before she met and heard the voice of
Jesus. False promises, shallow declarations of commitment,
and lies of love. Used over and over, it might seem as though
she had the uncanny ability to attract losers who ruined her
life again and again. But then that hot, ordinary afternoon,
Jesus was waiting at the well.

And He is waiting to speak to you and me. Are we ready
to listen?

———————

How does my life reflect the fact that I do or don't believe
Jesus is waiting to speak to me?

What adjustments do I have to make in my *thinking* for me
to receive what Jesus has to say to me?

What adjustments do I have to make to my *schedule* to accommodate personal time listening for His voice?

The Lord is impressing on me today:

I want to share with the Lord today:

Chapter · 22 ·

The Voice That Gives New Life

Read Luke 7:11–15.
Reflect on these words from verse 13:

When the Lord saw her, his heart went out to her and he said, "Don't cry."

She had already lost her husband, and now her only son was taken by death. How tragically similar to events we read about in our own daily newspapers: drive-by shootings, war-torn nations, ethnic cleansing—all exacting their destructive menace and painful affliction. For far too many people in our world, tragedy is no stranger.

It's no wonder Jesus was moved with compassion toward this dear woman. Death had taken her husband, and now death had stolen her only son as well. And life wasn't offering anything in return. No other pain in all her life could possibly equal her grief at this moment.

With her future ruined and her hope shattered in a million terrible, mocking pieces, she had no choice but to follow her son's coffin to his grave site—yet without knowing that her pathway was to come across that of the Savior, Jesus. She couldn't have possibly known that the Giver of Life himself would come into her life that day. She didn't plan to meet Him; she didn't dress for an appointment with Him. She simply allowed herself to be swept up in the momentum of her personal grief, wanting to be with the dead body of her only son as long as possible.

But she did cross the path of Christ that day. And although life had taken much more than it could possibly give, Jesus gave her much more than she could possibly imagine.

He was moved by compassion, the Bible says. Pity, tenderness, and sympathy reached from the heart of the Son of God and found its focus on this hopeless woman. So touched was Jesus by the scene passing in front of Him that He couldn't stand to do nothing—His heart went out to her, the Bible says. And He said, "Don't cry."

We all know men who are uncomfortable with women's tears, but Jesus isn't one of those men. We've all heard people say, "I wish you'd stop crying like that. It's not helping, you know." But Jesus' tone was different. He could tell her to stop crying for a very good reason. He knew what was about to happen . . . for in the very next movement of His hand, He touched the coffin of the dead son, and immediately the pallbearers stood perfectly still. The next words Jesus spoke were not only to the dead son, but to the woman's shattered dreams, ruined future, and expired hope. "I say to you," Jesus said, "get up."

What would you do if Jesus' voice pierced through your pain and grief, and He gently said, "Don't cry"? What would your shattered dreams and dead hopes do if Jesus spoke directly to them and said, "Get up!"

Isn't He the same today as He was then? Doesn't He still appear from nowhere when we are on our funeral marches on the way to bury our dreams that now sour with the putrid smell of disappointment? Yes, He does. He really does.

Listen with your heart and hear Him speak to you. Imagine He has just come across your pathway today, and read the following words as if He were speaking them directly to you:

Don't cry, my daughter. I'm here, and I'm not going to let this ruin your life and shatter your hopes and dreams. I say to you, my heart is touched with your grief, and I say to those hopes and dreams, get up, live again. Life may have taken much more than it has given—but I offer you life that gives much more than it takes. Wipe your eyes, dear woman; weep no more. For I have

112

come to give you life, and life much more abundant than you could ever imagine. Let this life have what it will take, but I will return to you even more. Will you trust me for that? Will you let me touch the dead things in your life and bring them to life again?

If Jesus were to touch the dearest thing in my life that I thought was dead and even buried, what would it be?

And what does that particular thing represent to me? Hope? Future? Worth? Acceptance? Other:

If Jesus were to resurrect it, what changes would you expect to see in your life?

Immediately:

In the near future:

In the distant future:

Today God is impressing on me:

In a short statement of twenty words or less, summarize below what you have heard the Lord say to you during today's quiet time:

Chapter
· 23 ·

The Voice
That Calms

Read Mark 4:35–41.
Reflect on these words from verse 39 (KJV):

And he arose, and rebuked the wind, and said unto the sea, "Peace, be still."

As I write this (trying to make a deadline, of course) I'm in one of those overwhelming times. My grandchildren are visiting, I'm getting ready to leave for an extended visit in another part of the state, and I'm rearranging my office. I'm also coping with an unwelcome physical inconvenience, as well as preparing my heart to assist a friend in the last days of her husband's life. All this in addition to the demands of my regularly scheduled life! Stretched in every way possible by those who genuinely need me, I long for someone to calm the storm swirling through my home at this moment.

Somehow, I must find the peace I need to get all the necessary things done within the next few days, as well as reserve enough energy to manage what awaits me at the beginning of next week. Laundry, packing, estimating what materials and books I'll need, and wondering all the while if I'll be able to clean my refrigerator before I go. Extra responsibilities pull at me, as do the daily demands of meals and loose ends to tie up before I leave. Where is my peace? Where do I plug in for resource and assistance?

The words from the Gospels concerning Jesus' rebuking

115

of the wind and waves sound like a prescription written especially for me. How about you? Couldn't you use a little of Jesus' calming ability in the storms of your life, too?

In reading and rereading this passage, I have to chuckle inside. I know exactly how it feels to know Jesus is aboard, but from all appearances, He certainly must be fast asleep. Otherwise, I insist, He'd be doing something to help me out here!

I can only imagine if the howling winds and rocking boat didn't wake Him, how did the fearful disciples manage to do so? I know I would have grabbed Him by His clothes and shook Him until I saw His eyes open and I knew I had captured His full attention.

In the Williams' translation* of the Bible, verse 37 reads like this: "A furious squall of wind came up, and the waves were dashing over into the boat, so that it was fast filling." I've had more than my share of days like that, haven't you? Circumstances tossing first one crisis my way, then another. Decision after decision clamoring for my attention. Sometimes life comes at me as fast as a furious squall. Waves of details dash over into my life so fast that I feel as if I'll sink under the weight of it all.

Williams goes on in verse 39: "Then He aroused himself. . . ." Hallelujah! Jesus is awake after all! He isn't sleeping through my storm. Nor yours. He is fully awake.

"And," the Bible says, "He reproved the storm and said to the sea, 'Hush! Be still!' And the wind lulled, and there was a great calm."

I haven't heard the voice of the Lord speak to an actual foul-weather storm, but I have seen the results of those times when He has spoken into those foul-circumstance storms of my own life. Those times when I've called out to Him, and the confusion suddenly cleared up and the static within my own heart and mind quieted. Yes, Jesus himself has spoken into the rough seas of my experience, lulled my unsteady feelings, and brought great calm into my life.

And He did it with a single word: "Hush." Jesus still

---

*New Testament in the Language of the People (Chicago: Moody Press, 1963).

116

speaks the words, "Peace, be still." He will speak them for you, too. Listen.

———

In the following, put words or phrases that are appropriate to the present "storms" in your own life, and how you would like to see the Lord respond to your need.

But a furious squall of wind concerning _____ has come up, and waves of _____ are dashing into my _____, so overwhelming that I fear _____. So I wake Him and I say, "Master, is _____ no concern to you? Can't you see that I'm: _____

_____

_____

_____

Now He awakes, reproves the _____ and is saying to _____, "Peace, be still. Hush."

And, now, right now, I sense a great calm. Now I see Jesus turning to me and I hear Him say:

(What do you think Jesus is saying to you about the areas of concern you have expressed above?)

Then, in your own words, write whatever else you sense the Lord is impressing on you through this passage:

Chapter
· 24 ·

The Voice
That Comforts

Read Exodus 33:12–22.
Reflect on these words in verse 14:

> The LORD replied, "My Presence will go with you, and I
> will give you rest."

And also from verse 17:

> And the LORD said to Moses, "I will do the very thing you
> have asked, because I am pleased with you and I know
> you by name."

Can you imagine, not just talking to, but carrying on a
conversation with God himself? Upon first impression, it
may seem as if Moses is a bit bold in God's presence. His tone
seems edged with protest and doubt, if not fully argumen-
tative.

Perhaps we wouldn't be so brave. But keeping in mind
what God was asking Moses to do, if it were you or me in
Moses' shoes, standing face-to-face with God, would our
tone be any different?

God will be as patient with our need for reassurance of
His presence in our daily tasks as He was with Moses. I believe the responsibilities I find so overwhelming are just as
assigned to me as leading the children of Israel out of captiv-
ity was assigned to Moses. My duties may not be as dramatic
or noteworthy as those of Moses, but the people who depend

on me for ministry, encouragement, and support need me just as much as those on the brink of liberation needed Moses' leadership. Sometimes God needs human hands to do His work. His leadership has to be expressed in human servants: His ministry expressed through caring human instruments. That's where Moses, you, and I come in.

I can identify with Moses' questions and doubts. I've been there many times and probably will be again. Moses, as far as I'm concerned, wasn't just speaking for himself that day in the tent with God, but for me as well. I want to know those very things too. I want to ask God about my situation, too. I want to know who will go with me, or if I'm expected to go it alone. I want to remind God that the people I care for are also His people, and I wonder how they will know God assigned me to their care. And I need the same reassurance God gave Moses, that He will go with me and that the rest I need so desperately will be available to me. Furthermore, I want to say to God that I, too, can't do the things He's given me to do without an awareness of His presence and the assurance of His will.

I also need to know that God hasn't forgotten me and that my prayers are coming to His hearing ear and receptive heart. I need to know that God understands that, while the tasks ahead may not seem overwhelming to Him, they certainly are to me . . . and that there is a cleft in a rock somewhere where He can put me . . . and that I, too, can know experientially the covering of His hand.

How about you? Could you use the same reassurance that God gave Moses? Would you benefit by knowing that His presence goes with you and that He promises you rest and a place of safety?

Then think of these words as His personal message to you as well. Imagine His voice speaking directly to you as He says:

> *I know you by name, and I have given this task to you, not because I can't do it, but because I want you partnered in my work with me. I promise that I'm with you, that I have rest for you as you continue in my assigned place for you. I have heard what you have asked, and, in fact, every*

prayer you have ever even thought toward me will be answered as you trust me. I will cause my goodness to pass through your life, my radiance to shine through even your darkest moments and most difficult days. I am still the Giver of mercy and compassion—and I choose to give them liberally to you. I will provide a place near me where you can stand securely grounded on a rock-solid foundation. I have a cleft in a rock prepared to tuck you into as I move through the valleys and trials of your life. I—the I AM—am with you wherever you go and will enable you in whatever task I put before you.

———

After hearing this message, how has your trust level of God been affected?

How can you make sure to pay attention to His presence as you face your assigned responsibilities?

If God's voice is to be heard, what other voices need silencing while you listen to Him?

What prayers do I want and need to pray? (Write out your prayer below.)

Chapter · 25 ·

The Voice That Is With You Always

Read Matthew 28:28–20.
Reflect on these words in verse 20:

And surely I am with you always, to the very end of the age.

Circle any words from the lists below that make each word or phrase more meaningful for you.

Surely
undoubtedly, doubtlessly, unquestionably, positively, absolutely, beyond question, beyond a doubt, beyond the shadow of a doubt, certainly, decidedly, definitely, assuredly

I am
Jesus, the Son of God; my Savior, our Blessed Redeemer; the Author and Finisher of my faith; my Blessed Advocate; my Good Shepherd; the Lamb of God; the Light of the World; the Lord of All; the Lord of Glory; the Bright and Morning Star; the Lord of my Righteousness; the Prince of my Peace; my True Light; the Word

with you
alongside me; in my daily company; my companion; accompanying me; attending me; keeping care of me

always
all the time; every time; on every occasion; without exception; constantly; regularly; repeatedly, continually; incessantly; uninterruptedly; day in, day out; unfailingly; forever; eternally; even today; forever and ever

to the very end.
He will not let me muddle in the middle; He will not leave me in the lurch; He will not do anything less than see me clear through this; no matter how long it takes; until I finally lay aside my earthly burdens and responsibilities; until it's finished—over!

Now, as if the Lord were speaking directly to you, listen to these words:

Little child, I know you've been walking a road that seems to exact from you much more than it returns. But you've not been alone when your strength has given way to exhaustion, when your faith has been shattered, and your emotions rubbed raw. I haven't left you, not even for a moment. I'm the One who has attended you in your sleep, seen to it that you've gotten a minute of relief, or a moment of laughter, just in time to save you from total collapse. You haven't been alone, be sure of that. I Am the One who has prompted that kind word from a total stranger as well as a trusted friend. It is my hand that has touched you in the warm embraces, the little notes or phone calls from friends. And I will continue. My promise is as true for you as it was when I uttered it to my disciples and followers, when I, too, walked a path that took more than it gave. But you see, because I chose that pathway, I not only know how you feel, I know you! And you, too, will someday see the reward. Don't give up now. We're almost there!

Today God is impressing on me:

I have shared with the Lord:

In a paragraph or two, summarize below the most significant thing the Lord has said to you during this section of listening to His voice.

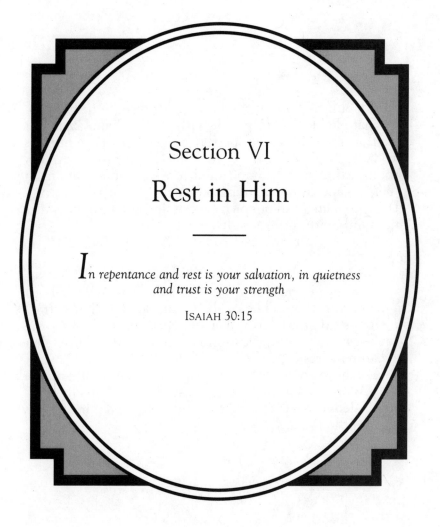

Section VI

Rest in Him

---

*In repentance and rest is your salvation, in quietness
and trust is your strength*

Isaiah 30:15

THE BIBLE SAYS that the Lord gives strength to His people, that He blesses His people with peace (Psalm 29:11). It says that He will keep in perfect peace him whose mind is steadfast, because he trusts in Him (Isaiah 26:3). And it promises that in repentance and rest we find salvation, in quietness and trust our strength (Isaiah 30:15). Yet we struggle, try to manage in our own energy, and exhaust our bodies and minds with futile activity.

"I can't rest now," we protest. "When this is over," we argue, "then I'll rest."

How wrong we are when we use such logic. When this is over we won't need rest, we'll have it then. We need rest right now, in the middle of the circumstances that extract much more than we have to give with no promise of return. Maybe we can't take a vacation from our responsibilities, but we can have rest.

For the next five days, let the Holy Spirit illuminate God's Word to you in new and restful ways. Let Him personally deliver the rest you have looked for and minister His peace in the process.

Chapter
· 26 ·

Trusting the
God of Our
Past, Present,
and Future

Read Psalm 116:1–7.
Reflect on these words from verse 7:

> *Be at rest once more, O my soul, for the LORD has been good to you.*

How tempting it is to look back at all our shortcomings and failures. Troubles imprint vivid memories within our minds, and old hurts haunt the hidden recesses of our hearts, just waiting to be recalled in times of stress and struggle. It makes handling present challenges difficult, if not impossible, when we look back or recall past hurts and regrets. Dealing with the past can drain us of the precious energy we need to handle the present. And the future? Forget about making plans and setting goals—there's hardly enough stamina to make it through today!

Many of us have been there, stuck in present situations and overwhelming responsibilities, carrying the weight of yesterday into tomorrow. A fresh start? Not much chance of that, we tell ourselves.

But then a passage like Psalm 116 comes to our attention. And what a message of hope it brings! Furthermore, it has some interesting instructional benefit as well. Let's look at it more closely.

Notice all the words that refer to the past: "He heard my voice; he heard my cry for mercy; He turned his ear to me."

These all refer to an experience when God helped before—in past struggles and stressful times. All through this passage, we see reference after reference that first refers to the past, then immediately refers to the future. See what I mean in verse two. Because of what I experienced in the past (God turned His ear to me), *I will* (referring to the future) *call on Him as long as I live* (distant future).

When a person recalls the past and then finds the strength to look to the future, he is living in the present. The present is the threshold between the past and the future. It is the pivotal point, the transition, the bridge. It is also where we are standing at this moment. It is where I live as I type these words into my little portable computer, and it's where you live as you read them months, perhaps years, later.

The interesting thing to note here is while you and I may take a deep, quick inhale before we utter the words, "Not again! I've been through this before," David didn't. We may moan, "What's next?" David the Psalmist exclaimed, "God helped me before (in the past); He heard me before. He'll help me now (in the present); He'll hear me now. And I can be sure He'll help me later on (in the future)."

Look again at these words from verses 3–6:

"The cords of death entangled me, the anguish of the grave came upon me; I was overcome by trouble and sorrow. Then I called on the name of the LORD: 'O LORD, save me!' " Past tense. "The LORD is gracious and righteous; our God is full of compassion. The LORD protects the simple-hearted." Present tense! The Lord *is* . . . God *is* . . . the Lord *protects*—now, today, this moment. Therefore, with yesterday's sour experiences covered by His love and grace, and His strength pouring into me today, I can say with assurance He will be there tomorrow—and so will I!

Now I can say with confidence, "Be at rest once more, O my soul, for the Lord has been good to you."

How do we manage to latch on to this rest? By standing on God's Word and knowing from experience that He's been good to us in the past, He longs to be good to us in the present, and we can count on His goodness in the future. It's settled, and I can now discipline myself to quiet my soul, no matter what I face today. I can apply God's precious Word

to my emotions, my stubborn will, and my fearful thoughts.
I can claim the comfort of His Word to cover my sick and
restless soul. In other words, I can rest.

And so can you.

Think of the Lord saying these words to you:

> *Remember when I took care of you before? Did I leave
> you without comfort? Did I leave you to handle the pressures
> all alone? Haven't I been there whenever you called upon
> me? Haven't I met you in unexpected ways and places in the
> past? Surely I'm not about to abandon you now. Only listen
> to my Word, remember my faithfulness, and recall my good-
> ness. Then take for yourself whatever it is you need for this
> day and for the days to come. I've been there for you before,
> I'm here now, and I'll be there later. So speak to your own
> soul and tell it the Master says to be at rest, for the Lord is
> good to you.*

Recall a time when the Lord met your need in the past.

How can you draw confidence in His care for the present
from that experience?

How can you know the Lord will be with you in the days and
years to come?

What is the Lord impressing on you right now?

How would you like to respond to what the Lord is impressing on you?

Further thoughts and prayers:

Chapter · 27 ·

God's Transcending Peace

Read Philippians 4:4–7.
Reflect on these words from verse 7:

And the peace of God, which transcends all understanding, will guard your hearts and your minds in Christ Jesus.

Nobody understands it perfectly. Everybody forgets once in a while that they can experience it every moment. That's why it is good to be reminded. We can have His peace—not hope for it or know it will come someday—no, you can have it right now, today.

Earlier in this book, I referred to my friend whose husband was dying. As I write this chapter her husband has passed away, and we are preparing for his burial service. In all the difficulty, it has come to my attention how many loose ends a person leaves when he dies. No matter what, we don't finish this life, we quit it. Let me explain.

My friend's daughter, Michelle, and her dad had several areas of misunderstanding between them, and having to leave some of these issues unresolved has been especially painful to Michelle. Even having close to a year's notice that her father would probably die of this disease didn't help. Time after time, when Michelle tried to bridge the gap, he remained uncommunicative and distant in many areas, yet demanded closeness in others. As this painful relationship ends, she is left with unfinished business, and now to her pain has been added the sense of loss and loose ends.

"Should I have tried harder?" she might ask herself. "Could I have been more sensitive to him when he wanted to talk, and did I miss opportunities with him?" Maybe she has even said, "I just don't understand it."

Right now, Michelle needs more than understanding. At best, our own understanding is not much more than speculation. I can offer theories and ideas, but more than anything you and I could possibly offer, Michelle needs God's peace. I can't identify with her, because my father and I were close, and our accounts were settled long before he died. But I have other relationships in which I've experienced dead ends and blank walls, with no choice but to leave certain issues unresolved and ends untidy and loose.

That's why the words of our reflection verse are so meaningful at times like this. The question has to be asked, if God's Word can transcend even our understanding, what else can it transcend?

Transcend means that it exceeds what we can understand, that it's even better than our understanding. Far superior to our way of thinking and reasoning, God's peace fills in the cracks of our ability to comprehend our situation. Even the most difficult and crazy day can be saturated with God's peace. How? I honestly don't know. The concept of God's peace is beyond my understanding. However, it isn't beyond my ability to accept it.

I'm not sure what you face today, but, like Michelle, is it possible you need God's peace, too? He has promised it to Michelle, and He has promised it to you. It can be your reality today—better, preferable, and a far superior choice to your own understanding, wouldn't you agree?

And the result? A mind guarded against endless regret-filled thoughts and painful memories of failure and frustration. Best of all, a heart free of anger and bitterness over the futility of the loose ends left behind.

God's peace isn't exclusive to Michelle and me—it's offered to you, too. No matter what you're responsible for today, no matter how much life extracts from you without any return, God's peace is held out to you by the tender hand of your loving heavenly Father. Won't you let His peace make a difference in your life today? Take it; it's yours. And it's all a part of His plan to give you the rest you need so much.

Think of the Lord speaking these words to you:

> *Take it, my daughter. I offer you my peace. Let it surpass the questions and doubts that have assaulted you in the night. Let it flood your heart with rest, and rejoice in me. You don't have to struggle to understand and get all the answers in order for you to have peace. No, my peace can transcend all you have labored to understand. Here it is— it's yours.*

————————

What do you think you have to understand in order to get a handle on your circumstances and have peace?

How does this prevent you from having rest in the middle of your situation?

What do you think you'd lose control of if you ceased struggling for understanding?

What or who would be affected if you let yourself have peace in the midst of the demands of your life?

How?

What is it that God seems to be impressing on you about His peace today?

What would you like to share with Him about that?

Further thoughts and prayers:

Chapter · 28 ·

A Royal Legacy

Read John 14:23–27.
Reflect on these words from verse 27:

> *Peace I leave with you; my peace I give you. I do not give to you as the world gives. Do not let your hearts be troubled and do not be afraid.*

As a child I fancied myself a princess—the pretend daughter of an imaginary wealthy king who would someday leave his fortune, his kingdom, and, of course, all the royal jewels to me. My imagination carried me far away in grand style, where I could enjoy all the privileges of one born into royalty. Unfortunately, at the most incredible peak of my highest daydreams, my mother usually called me to do some undignified task, such as carrying out potato peelings or shaking rugs. In a second I was jolted back to the reality of my lowly status as the daughter of hard-working parents who often struggled to make ends meet.

Now, as an adult, I discover that I *am* the daughter of a king! And while my legacy here on earth doesn't include fine and expensive robes or diamond-studded jewelry, it does include something far more needed and practical—God, through Jesus, left me the legacy of His peace.

No, it doesn't help me buy my way out of tight situations, but it gives me rest and peace in them. I can't order a royal regiment to protect me from the onslaught of the enemy of my soul, and I can't hire replacements to run my household or fulfill my responsibilities to my husband and family. However, I can draw on the reserve of God's rest, the abundance of His mercy, and the unending supply of His peace.

When I receive my inheritance of peace, I no longer have to be suffocated by the needs of others, run ragged by demands on my time and energy, or be beat to a frazzle by my perception of what I should be able to accomplish. When I accept my legacy of God's peace, I am strong in the face of fear, calm in the midst of turmoil, and faith-filled in the presence of uncertainty.

What's more, this is your legacy, too. He didn't leave it only to me. It's not as though I picked a winning lottery number and got the whole pot to keep for myself. It is a shared legacy. He left it to His body—for us all to share in equally. Not because we are more faithful than others, but because we are His children. Not because we have more talent, commitment, or have put in more hours of service, but for the simple fact that we belong to Him. We are His children—His family—and He left us something when He went to be with the Father. He left us His peace. And what's more, He intends that we take advantage of it. We don't have to wait until we "come of age"—as the royal heir of some earthly kingdom would have to. No, the *moment* we become His children we inherit His legacy.

But, of course, like any other inheritance, the heirs must lay claim to their portion. And you can, you know. By the blood of Jesus you can prove your identity and your legal title to His legacy of peace. By His resurrection you can live, by His ascension you can hope, and by His return someday very soon you can step forward as part of the royal family. And *today* you can spend this portion of your full inheritance— you can have His peace.

The world says you have to have all your problems solved and all your relationships negotiated successfully to have peace. They say you have to have all your bills paid and two new cars parked in your garage. The world says you have to be thin, beautiful, physically fit, and married to a handsome, successful husband, and have healthy, happy, well-behaved children. And, sadly, these prerequisites for worldly rest do not offer peace, but despair. Not happiness, but hopelessness. The simple, devastating fact is *the world can't deliver what it promises.*

Not so with Jesus. He delivers much more than He ever asks, and He never demands anything without first providing whatever we need to accomplish what He asks of us. He makes good on all His promises. So depend on it, my friend. When God promises you that Jesus has left you His legacy of peace, you can count on the fact that His peace is yours; that He will lead you into His rest; that He isn't requiring you to manage peace and rest on your own, but instead offers to give it to you.

Think of the Lord saying these words directly to you:

> *I have seen the load you carry and the burdens you bear; I feel the concern you live with every day. I know what disturbs you and keeps you from walking in the center of my peace. Will you listen to my Word and believe that I anticipated your need for peace? I knew you would need it—right at this time and in this very situation. Give me your concerns and lay your burdens on my shoulders. Take my peace upon you. Let it affect the pace at which you walk, the responses that so quickly escape your mouth, and the decisions that you face. Let my peace permeate your heart and mind. Let me give you something no one else can give—let me give you peace.*

———

What prevents you from taking advantage of the peace that Jesus intentionally left you?

When do you feel the need for God's peace the most?

When do you feel the lack of it the most?

How would your life change if you experienced more of His peace on a daily basis?

Further thoughts and prayers:

Chapter · 29 ·

To All Who Are Weary

Read Matthew 11:28–29.
Reflect on these words from verse 29:

"Come to me, all you who are weary and burdened, and I will give you rest."

"I need a break!" she cried while I held her in my arms. "I just don't know what to do anymore. I'm so tired. You'd think I would know how to be an overcomer by now! After all, I've been a Christian for more than thirty years! I've just got to get hold of myself. Somehow, I've just got to get a handle on this!"

I've been there, too. How about you? My circumstance isn't even close to being the same one my tearful friend is going through, but I know just how she feels and have even cried out the same words to her on occasion. *Time out*, we think. *That's what I need.* And, while it is true that a recess would be welcome and wonderful—what happens to us when it doesn't come? What happens when a difficult situation doesn't give us even a momentary respite?

Sometimes in the most difficult situations we find the many facets and difficult areas of life rubbing against each other, creating a friction that seems unbelievably challenging and even threatening. We find ourselves being pressured to perform in one area, submit in another. Take charge in still a different situation and give up in something else.

Nothing seems to fit; everything seems out of balance. And if that isn't enough, still another problem arises and we're called on to be strong and take charge, or to yield and give up control.

These tension-filled areas of our life are charged with emotional electricity as the different roles we play and responsibilities we carry bump and rub against each other. And it can wear us out. Yet right in the middle of it all, the Lord's invitation is "come." "Come to me," He says, "and get some rest."

"Rest?" we protest. "You must be kidding. Who's going to fill in for me while I'm taking this *rest*? What I need right now is a new burst of strength and energy. A new dose of enthusiasm and a double dose of determination." So we take a deep breath of resolve and plow ahead. *After all, we reason, whatever energy the Lord doesn't provide, my own adrenaline will cover. Somehow I'll make it through this awful day, and tonight when I put my head on my pillow, then I'll think about the Lord and . . .*

Hold it!

"But," we cry, "what do you expect me to do? I've got this demanding responsibility, and what about that other situation? And what about. . . ?"

Hold it! I said. Just, hold it! Look closer at this passage.

"Come to me, all you who are weary and burdened, and I will give you rest."

We're not talking about a get-away-from-it-all kind of rest here. We're talking about a God-given rest. Not just to regroup and regear for yet another long exhausting day, but the kind of rest that meets us where we are, that sees us through endless, demanding, sleepless nights. Not a good long vacation after the impossible situation has been handled or solved by our own self-provided, superhuman effort, but a right-in-the-middle-of-it rest provided by a gracious and merciful touch of God.

Jesus said, "Come." Simple, huh? A common one-syllable word. "Come." Simple, but so difficult sometimes. I'm living proof of just how difficult this concept is, and so are you. And so is most of the rest of the body of Christ. Yet, if we would hear this invitation as personal, and significant for the challenge of this very moment, we'd drop everything and run toward His inviting voice.

So before you make the mistake of beating yourself up for not answering this invitation sooner, remember this: as you turn your ear toward the voice of Jesus whispering, "Come. I will give you rest," your struggles, problems, and endlessly trying circumstances will not stop screaming for your attention. They have a strange magnetism that will tug and pull at you. The friction in our lives generates an invisible industrial-strength power to prevent us from hearing and responding to the tender beckoning invitation of our Lord.

A break? You bet. That is exactly what we all need. But not necessarily the God-intervention variety we normally wish and pray for. No, it is our own welcoming of the Master that is needed—right here in the middle of this awful tug-of-war. And when we do, He comes with that coveted, essential rest we all long for. "Come," He still whispers. "Come."

"But how do I do this?" you might ask. By making a simple decision. By responding to the invitation to come to Jesus for the rest He offers in spite of all the problems and perplexities you face at the moment. But remember, the responsibilities or problems will not go away while you receive the gift of rest from Jesus. For His rest is not to give you an escape. Rather, it is to equip.

Read Matthew 11:29 again: "Take my yoke upon you and learn from me." That is the answer. This is the wisdom you need. But first you must accept His invitation to receive the rest He alone can give—*then* you will find the answers you need.

Now ask yourself: When I'm weary and burdened how does my life reflect the fact that I believe in this invitation of the Lord?

Then, as if the Lord were speaking directly to you, listen to these words:

> Come to me all you who toil and carry burdens, and I, yes I, will lead you into rest. Put on my yoke and learn from me, for I am gentle and humble in heart, and you will find rest for your souls, for the yoke I offer is easy to wear, and the load I ask is light to bear.* I will carry this load in tandem with you if you'll only let me. I have given the invitation, but you must accept and come. It's okay to come bringing whatever burdens you carry at this moment. You will soon be renewed, refreshed, and rested. I promise—and I await you.

Today God is impressing on me that . . .

I need to share with the Lord that . . .

The overwhelming responsibilities that are wearing me out are:

I could handle them much better if . . .

A particular challenge for me today is . . .

---

*Williams, *New Testament in the Language of the People* (Chicago: Moody Press, 1963).

In a short statement of twenty words or less, summarize below what you think the Lord has said to you during today's quiet time:

Chapter
• 30 •

Beside Quiet Waters

Read Psalm 23.
Reflect on these words from verses 2 and 3:

He makes me lie down in green pastures, he leads me beside quiet waters, he restores my soul.

Last night I was enjoying a quiet dinner out with some close friends, when suddenly I caught myself feeling guilty. Why? Because I wasn't where I thought somebody needed me to be. Then it occurred to me—I was having a green pasture experience, a brief respite beside quiet waters. Responsibilities awaited me, of course, but I realized at that moment I was *supposed* to be enjoying a break from the hectic demands of my life. God was giving me some rest and relaxation to refresh me before I had to step back into those demands.

Are you like me? Do you feel guilty whenever you have a little time to yourself? The last time you shopped for clothes, did you just pick them off the rack and head for home, or did you try them on leisurely? When was the last time you felt you could take the time to read a recipe book or even the labels on the grocery store shelves? Too busy? Too much in a hurry? Too many things to do?

God has made green pastures, my friend. He has quiet waters for you to enjoy. Not later, not someday—now. Far too often, quiet moments offered in the middle of responsibility go unnoticed, don't they?

Radios blast the bad news of our cities and country as we run from one appointment to another. Even our bathrooms are filled with reading material. We quickly shower instead of soaking in the tub. We have let household conveniences affect the way we think—everything must happen microwave quick and be handled as easily as automatic washers are to run.

But life isn't as simple as that. Our problems can't be placed in the microwave and processed in a few seconds. They can't be sorted like towels and play clothes, then stuffed into a washing machine for solving.

No, life is hard. Your life and mine. And it doesn't appear as if it will get any easier anytime soon. Yet God's Word says that He would like us to take it easier. The Bible paints us a picture that we would admire on a calendar or a friendship card, but we can't imagine relaxing like that in reality. A lush green-pastured scene, with a laid-back easygoing shepherd tending a few woolly sheep, and a cool, unpolluted stream gurgling nearby. Can you picture it?

How does God make us lie down in those green pastures when our lives are so full of rocky obstacles and filled with weeds needing to be pulled right this minute? This book is only one of the ways God would offer that to you. Quiet moments spent with Him don't have to occur only at a special retreat or at some exotic vacation spot. God offers green pastures right here, right now.

His green pastures, His still waters, grow and flow surrounded by the noise and confusion of your life and the demanding responsibilities you carry. He not only offers the out-in-the-country type of "pastoral" experiences, but also the rooftop-garden-in-the-middle-of-the-city type. Not just rural, away-from-it-all settings, but right here, in-the-middle-of-it-all moments of rest and restoration.

It has been my hope and prayer that this book will have taught you much more than I have written; that when applied to your difficult situation, your heaviest responsibility, and your unending cycle of being needed, you will have received more insight than I could have possibly imagined. I dream someday of meeting each of you face-to-face and laughing about the demands that threatened to finish us off but didn't. And most of all, for those of you who find that life often takes much more than it gives, I pray that you have discovered God's care for you at a deeper level than you ever dreamed possible, and that the people in your care are benefiting as well.

Can you point to one chapter or concept in this book and say, "That's what made the difference to me. That's what made this book worth the effort it took to read it."? What is it that made the difference to you?

How has this book helped you to understand others who are in the same or similar situation you are?

In what ways has God met you during these days studying these verses and concepts?

How is your life different because of what you learned or studied here?

What has God seemed to impress on you the most?

What one thing do you still need to share with Him?

What other thoughts and prayers do you now have the courage to think or pray?

Now, imagine Jesus speaking these words directly to you:

> These have been precious moments for me, too, my cherished one. I have longed to say these things to you for more days than you think. I understand the pressures of your life and the responsibilities you carry. I promise you that I'll not permit anything beyond your strength to endure, your ability to carry, and my power to sustain. I have heard your prayers, seen your tears, and been touched by the weariness in your voice and the tiredness I have seen in your eyes. Just remember this: I haven't abandoned you. Look to me for strength, and while life may take more than it gives, you have yet to receive all I have prepared and all I have waiting for you. No effort will be wasted, my love; no extension of yourself will be unnoticed. I am here . . . I see . . . I know. And I understand. Trust me. For you cannot possibly know all that I am doing and will do on your behalf. I will sustain you when you're beyond tired. I will lift you when no one else thinks to encourage you. I will heal the hurt you carry and lighten the load that rests upon your shoulders. When others prove unfaithful, I promise to remain faithful. Enter my rest, my child—then take my hand. I love you more than you could ever know.

What would you like to say in response?

Leader's Notes

GROUP GUIDELINE SUGGESTIONS

As mentioned at the beginning of this book, if this study is used in a group setting, members should study the five entries or each section throughout the week in preparation for discussion at the weekly meeting. In this way, the material is covered in six weeks. A group may decide to spend more or less time on a given section depending on the needs of the participants. Discussion questions are included at the end of these leader's notes.

A good general group approach to this study is one of personal investigation and shared responses. Discussion questions will help bring out even more insight into application for personal growth.

In the course of covering the material, some very private areas of personal discovery may be exposed or brought to mind. A leader should not expect, nor force, everyone to participate each time or respond to each discussion question. Do encourage even the slightest participation with affirmative comments, regardless of the contribution.

Because this is a responsive study, there are no wrong answers. The nature of the study tends to get to the heart of many emotional issues. Some people in your group may desperately need a listening ear, and a correction from you may discourage them from participating in the discussion, or even keep them from attending your group again. Allow the Holy Spirit to do the correcting and a deep work of patience and sensitivity in you, the leader.

Once in a while, there will be a member of a group who monopolizes the conversation or goes off on a tangent. If so, very carefully approach that person afterward and ask if you can be of help individually. There may be times during the study when a person may genuinely come to a breakthrough, drawing the attention of the group to herself and her needs exclusively. That would be the exception, however, and not the rule.

If someone in your group asks a question, don't take the sole responsibility for having an answer. Allow others in the group to contribute. If you do give an answer, give it after others have spoken.

There are three basic group rules that you should follow without fail:

1. *Start and end on schedule.* Everyone is busy, so set your meeting times and stick to them. One and one half hours generally works well for evening groups. Daytime groups may wish to meet for a little longer. Sunday school groups need to meet within an assigned schedule. Actual study and discussion should take only a portion of the meeting time. Fellowship and sharing prayer requests help develop strong bonds within your group. Make time for that to happen.

2. *Begin and end with prayer.* The opening prayer can be a simple offering by one person asking God's blessing on your time together. You may feel the need in your group to have additional time for prayer concerns or needs of the group. (One effective way to handle this is to have everyone write down the name of the person they are concerned for and a very brief statement about the need on a small piece of paper. The slips are put into a basket and redistributed to the group. Each person then offers a

sentence prayer concerning the request they have drawn from the basket.) Closing prayers should be centered around the needs that have arisen related to the study and discussion. Bring the meeting to a close with your own prayer.

3. *Involve everyone*. Many of the issues covered in this study are of a personal nature. Depending on the amount of abuse and misunderstanding your group members have experienced, some may not be ready to discuss the issues they are dealing with. However, during the fellowship time, the time of praying for others, and the ongoing study, seek to build trust and encourage them to open their hearts and share with the group. Find a way to involve even the most reserved people in a way that is comfortable and safe for them.

Discussion times can be rich and rewarding for everyone—that is, everyone who gets to share and discuss. The size of the group somewhat determines the opportunities for sharing. A group of six members is ideal, but a group as large as ten can work. When the group reaches ten, consider the advantages of dividing into smaller groups of three or four for at least a portion of the sharing and discussion time.

Discussion Questions

Orientation—Introduction
You may find it helpful to have an orientation meeting before you begin a group study of this book. Such a meeting will allow members of the group to have opportunity to look over the book and to prepare for the first discussion and sharing time.

The following questions will help your group members get off to a good start and understand what you expect to accomplish in the study.

1. Many people have difficulty fitting a daily quiet time into their routine. In what ways have you tried to do this? What ways have worked for you, and what ways have not worked?

2. Everyone experiences difficulties in their lives at times. For some, those difficult times never seem to end, and life begins to take much more than it gives. Has this been your experience? What are some of the ways you have tried to cope? Have they been successful or unsuccessful?

3. When we read a book or embark on a new study, not every illustration or example fits our own particular situation. Yet we might find such an illustration to be helpful in some way. Why do you think this is true?

4. Read aloud the introduction to each study section, then discuss what some of your expectations are concerning this study.

Assignment

Everyone should first read "How to Use This Book" at the beginning of the book. Each day for five days before you meet again, read and respond to each of the devotional studies in Section I, "Come Into His Presence." (Before each meeting, members should read and study the five chapters for the section to be discussed at the next meeting.)

Section I: Come Into His Presence

To begin the first study, read together the introduction to the section. Use the following questions as models or thought-starters for group discussion:

1. In our busy lives are we more apt to hear God's voice as a welcome interlude or an unwelcome intrusion?

2. Have you been taught to seek God's presence as a part of your daily life in Christ? Comment.

3. In Chapter Two, the idea of masks, or facades, is discussed as a natural response to God's voice speaking to us. How do you see yourself in this regard? And how do you let down your masks and become real in His presence?

4. How did you respond to Chapter Three's questions about making time to consider "but as for me"?

5. What are some of the ways we manage to avoid or convince ourselves we don't *need* to make time for quietness with the Lord?

6. What are some of the ways we manage to convince ourselves that we are *prevented* from making time for quietness with the Lord?
7. How do some of your normal duties and responsibilities take you away from God rather than closer to Him?
8. Please comment on the performance review from the end of Chapter 5. How would you rate yourself?
9. What does this invitation of entering God's presence mean to you?
10. What are some of the ways you can make a place in your life and busy schedule for that to happen?

Section II: Let Down Your Guard
Read together the introduction to the section and then discuss the following:

1. When life takes more than it gives, it can become a natural defense mechanism to put our guard up. Do you react like this in difficult times? Why?
2. When we keep our guard up continually, how does that prevent us from truly experiencing God's presence? His strength?
3. Do you "hang on" as if all of life's problems and circumstances depended on you? When did that begin? How?
4. What are some of the emotional feelings you experience when you consider the idea of being totally vulnerable to God?
5. Have you ever let your responsibilities or an overcrowded schedule delay, or even indefinitely postpone, your quiet time? With what result?
6. Do you tend to judge God's mercy based on the mercy you have *received* from others? Comment. Do you tend to judge God's mercy based on the mercy *you have* for others? Comment.
7. How is God's mercy different from any that we've ever received or known before?
8. How can the members of this study group pray for you this week?

Section III: Open Your Heart
Read together the introduction to the section and then discuss the following:

1. At one time or another, most of us have opened our hearts to someone in need, only to find they have set up housekeeping on our doorstep, either literally or emotionally. How can that experience harden our hearts toward God?

2. Can you ever recall a time when you patted yourself on the back for praying when you heard God met someone else's need? How did the Lord reveal to you your pride in that experience?

3. In the last several days, has the Lord spotlighted any areas of self-reliance that you need to deal with? How can we avoid the sin of self-reliance without going overboard and becoming totally dependent and helpless?

4. Is there some deep, even hidden hesitancy to being totally open with God and pouring out our needs as David did in Psalm 38:9? How so?

5. How can we allow Jesus into the "inner chambers" of our hearts? What are some of the ways we keep Him out?

6. Read John 14:23. Can you say, "Come on in, Lord Jesus, make yourself at home"?

7. Your personal circumstances probably have not changed very much since we began this study. Have they gotten worse?

8. How have *you* changed? In your thinking? In your perspective? In the way you approach your circumstances?

9. If God were to alter your situation as a result of a deep change within you, what do you think that change might be?

10. How can we pray for each other more effectively this week?

Section IV: Let God Love You
Read together the introduction to the section and then discuss the following:

1. In what ways do you easily slip into depending on your own strength, ingenuity, or resourcefulness to handle your challenging responsibilities?

2. How does that happen?

3. First John, chapter 4, connects our ability to love others

with our personal experience and understanding of God's love. How does that differ from the popular thought that we must first love ourselves before we can love others?

4. What answer do you come up with when you ask yourself the question, "Have I tried to love others without experiencing God's love for me first?"

5. How does the concept *not that I love God, but that He loves me* change how you receive God's love?

6. Recall and share with this group a time you sensed God's perfect love superseding your own imperfect love for Him and others: a specific instance when God's love broke through circumstances and your imperfection and showered you with attention.

7. How has the concept of this section changed how you view God's love for you? How has it changed the way you love others?

Section V: Listen to His Voice
Read together the introduction to the section and then discuss the following:

1. Do we really believe God's Word?

2. Can we actually accept as fact the concept that God desires to speak to and with His people as He has from the beginning?

3. Can you accept the idea that God has something to say to you?

4. Is there a need for caution in this area? Explain.

5. How does my life reflect the fact that I believe Jesus is waiting to speak to me?

6. How does my life reflect the fact that sometimes I *don't* believe that Jesus can and will speak to me?

7. In a short statement summarize what you have heard the Lord say to you during this study.

8. Complete this sentence: A problem I'm having with the concept of hearing God is . . .
And this one: A problem I have in hearing God is . . .

9. Think of these words as His personal message to you. Imagine His voice speaking directly to you as He says:

I know you by name, and I have given this task to you,

157

not because I can't do it, but because I want you partnered in my work with me. I promise that I'm with you, that I have rest for you as you continue in my assigned place for you. I have heard what you have asked, and, in fact, every prayer you have ever even thought toward me will be answered as you trust me. I will cause my goodness to pass through your life, my radiance to shine through even your darkest moments and most difficult days. I am still the Giver of mercy and compassion—and I choose to give them liberally to you. I will provide a place near me where you can stand securely grounded on a rock-solid foundation. I have a cleft of a rock prepared to tuck you into as I move through the valleys and trials of your life. I—the I AM—am with you wherever you go and will enable you in whatever task I put before you.

If God were to say those things directly to you, how would your trust level of God be affected?

10. In what areas do you need prayer support from this group this week?

Section VI: Rest in Him
Read together the introduction to the section and then discuss the following:

1. How is the idea of God bringing rest to you (rather than you getting away to find it) new to you?
2. What changes inside you would help you draw from His rest and care right in the middle of your circumstance?
3. Read a dictionary definition of *transcend*. How does God's rest and peace transcend your situation?
4. Read aloud the last paragraph in Chapter 27 ("Think of the Lord speaking these words to you . . ."). Are those around you comfortable with your having such peace and rest? Are you?
5. What are the peace-robbers that try to take away the peace that Jesus intentionally left you?
6. When Jesus said, "Come to me all you who are weary and heavy laden," do you think of bringing Him those things that weigh you down, or of somehow getting rid of them first? How do you think those two ideas differ? And what results from each idea?

7. Read Psalm 23 aloud together. Then choose one person to read the paragraph at the end of Chapter 30 ("Think of Jesus saying to you . . .").
8. What one chapter or concept in this study made a difference to you? How?
9. Share with the group how God has met you during this study and group time.
10. What new skills are you working on but have not yet mastered, based on the concepts of this study? How can the group pray for you in the days and weeks to come?